TEACHER'S RESOURCE MASTERS

BLACKLINE MASTERS AND TEACHER'S MANUAL

W9-DAB-954

GRADE 5

SHARE
the
Music

McGRAW-HILL

SERIES AUTHORS

Judy Bond
Coordinating Author

René Boyer-Alexander

Margaret Campbelle-Holman

Marilyn Copeland Davidson
Coordinating Author

Robert de Frece

Mary Goetze
Coordinating Author

Doug Goodkin

Betsy M. Henderson

Michael Jothen

Carol King

Vincent P. Lawrence
Coordinating Author

Nancy L.T. Miller

Ivy Rawlins

Susan Snyder
Coordinating Author

**McGraw-Hill
School Division**

New York   Farmington

INTRODUCTION

This ***Teacher's Resource Masters*** book contains supplementary activities for ***Share the Music***.

The Resource Masters include the following:

- A variety of activities that reinforce or review concepts taught in the lessons. Some Resource Masters emphasize manipulative activities, while others offer written and aural activities.

- Listening maps that provide visual guidance for students as they listen to specific music selections. The listening maps help students identify melodic and rhythmic patterns, tone color, form, and other musical elements.

- Assessment questions for each unit. The assessment questions and music examples are recorded. Two recorded options are available for each question.

- Script for musical.

- Tools for Assessment, including portfolio and self-assessment forms.

- An answer key.

All Resource Masters may be duplicated for classroom use. Each is keyed into the Teacher's Edition. A line at the bottom of the Resource Master identifies the page in the Teacher's Edition with which the Resource Master is intended to be used.

For listening maps, teaching suggestions are provided on the back of the Resource Master.

ACKNOWLEDGMENTS

Grateful acknowledgment is given to the following authors, composers, and publishers. Every effort has been made to trace the ownership of all copyrighted material and to secure the necessary permissions to reprint these selections. In the case of some selections for which acknowledgment is not given, extensive research has failed to locate the copyright holders.

Plank Road Publishing for *Possibilities* (script), from the musical *Possibilities* by Teresa Jennings. Copyright © 1996 Plank Road Publishing, Inc. Used by permission of Teresa Jennings.

McGraw-Hill School Division ⚛
A Division of The McGraw-Hill Companies

McGraw-Hill School Division
Two Penn Plaza
New York, NY 10121

Printed in the United States of America

ISBN 0-02-295427-9 / 5

3 4 5 6 7 8 9 045 03 02 01

TABLE OF CONTENTS

		TEACHER'S EDITION page	RESOURCE MASTERS page

McGraw-Hill

McGraw-Hill

McGraw-Hill

Name _____

Let's Get Going!

Pat-clap to the beat as you listen to this speech piece. When it repeats, echo-speak the words, then echo-clap the rhythms on the next page.

By René Boyer-White

With a Swing

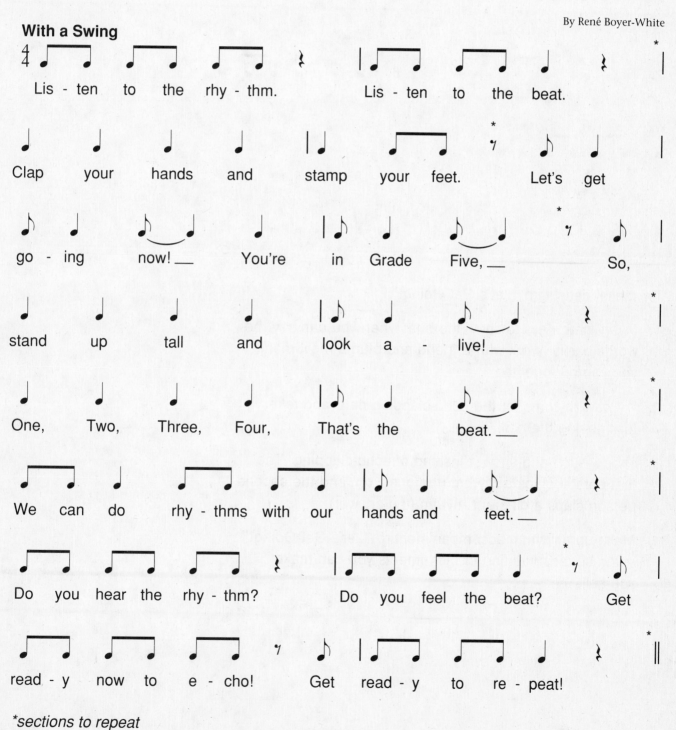

*sections to repeat

McGraw-Hill

Page 2

Echo-clap these patterns with "Let's Get Going!"

1. ♩ ♩ ♩ ♩

5. ♪♩ ♪♩ 𝄽

2. ♩ ♩ ♫ ♩

6. ♪♩ ♪♫ ♩

3. ♫ ♫ ♩ ♩

7. ♩. ♪♩ ♩

4. ♩ 𝄽 ♩ 𝄽

8. ♩ ♩ ♩ 𝄽

Try these ideas with "Let's Get Going!"

1. Invent new ways to show the beat when you can say the words easily. Work with a friend and plan a movement you can do together.

2. Try new rhythms for the echo-clapping part, and take turns being the new leader.

3. Try question-and-answer instead of echo-clapping. The first person claps a rhythm (the question) and the second person claps a different rhythm (the answer).

4. Make up a rhythm accompaniment to "Let's Get Going!" using sounds you find or instruments you can make yourself.

RESOURCE MASTER 1•2 Practice

Do Re Mi / G A B

Draw a line from the melody pattern on the staff to the matching pitch syllable names. Then sing the patterns with pitch syllables.

1.

a. *mi do re do*

2.

b. *re mi do mi*

3.

c. *re do mi do*

4.

d. *do do re mi*

5.

e. *mi re do mi*

Write the correct pitch letter names for each pattern using G A B.

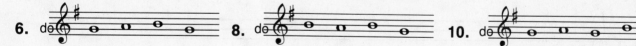
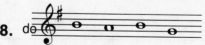
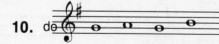

6. _____   8. _____   10. _____

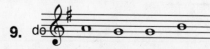

7. _____   9. _____

McGraw-Hill

(See answers at the back of this book.)

Do Re Mi in One More Key

Practice identifying F G A and G A B on the staff. Write the
pitch letter name and pitch syllable for each note in the
melodies. Sing or play the melodies.

1. do

___ ___ ___ ___

___ ___ ___ ___

4. do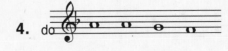

___ ___ ___ ___

___ ___ ___ ___

2. do

___ ___ ___ ___

___ ___ ___ ___

5. do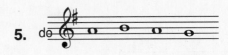

___ ___ ___ ___

___ ___ ___ ___

3. do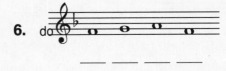

___ ___ ___ ___

___ ___ ___ ___

6. do

___ ___ ___ ___

___ ___ ___ ___

Write your own four-pitch melodies. Use F G A in the first
melody, and G A B in the second melody. Then play or sing
your melodies.

7. do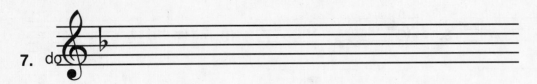

8. do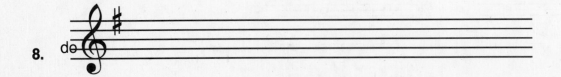

(See answers at the back of this book.)

McGraw-Hill

Name_____

Rhythm Training

1. Echo-clap these rhythms of quarter notes, eighth notes, and quarter rests. Work with a partner, or listen to the recording.

Circle the beat that changes from one example to the next.
For example, the difference between *a.* and *b.* is Beat 6.

2. Circle the rhythms containing four beats.

3. Fill in the blank spaces with  or
    Each rhythm should have four beats.

4. Clap or play one of the rhythms given above. Tell the class which rhythm you are going to clap, then ask them to name the rhythms you used in the blank spaces.

5. Create your own four-beat rhythm using ♩, ♫ or ♪
    Then practice it with a friend.

_____   _____   _____   _____

(See answers at the back of this book.)

Percussion Stars

Clap the rhythm in each star. Each rhythm is four beats long.
Do a clap-slide on the half notes.

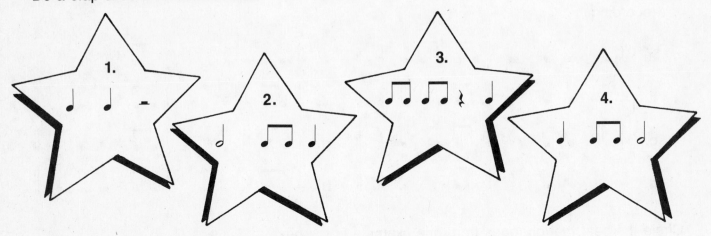

Write one of the rhythm patterns in each box. The same
pattern may be used more than once.

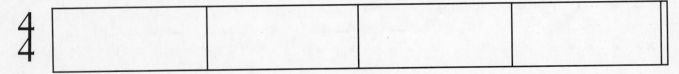

Listen to the rhythm patterns created by the other groups.
Can you identify the order of the stars they used? Combine
two or more patterns that were created and play them at the
same time.

Say this speech piece using rhythms you know.

Mer-cu-ry, Ve - nus, Earth, Mars, Ju - pi - ter, and Sat - urn.

Next come U - ra - nus, and Nep - tune and Plu - to.

Mer-cu-ry, Ve - nus, Earth, Mars, Ju - pi - ter, and Sat - urn.

Use with page 42. • Grade 5

Check It Out

1. Which rhythm do you hear?

a. [music notation]

b. [music notation]

c. [music notation]

d. [music notation]

2. Choose the melodic direction that you hear.

   a. [arrow up]   b. [arrow down]   c. [arrow down then up]   d. [arrow right]

3. Choose the melodic direction that you hear.

   a. [arrow up]   b. [arrow down]   c. [arrow down then up]   d. [arrow right]

4. Choose the melodic direction that you hear.

   a. [arrow up]   b. [arrow down]   c. [arrow down then up]   d. [arrow right]

5. Which example shows the pitches you hear?

   a. [music staff]   b. [music staff]   c. [music staff]   d. [music staff]

6. Which example shows the pitches you hear?

   a. [music staff]   b. [music staff]   c. [music staff]   d. [music staff]

(See answers at the back of this book.)

RESOURCE MASTER 1•7 Creative Assessment

Make a Melody

Follow these steps to create a melody.

1. Cut out the boxes on the dotted lines.

2. Choose rhythms using ♩, ♫ or 𝄽 to fill four measures in 𝄴 meter. The last beat should be a quarter rest.

3. Play the first two measures on a percussion instrument or found sound. Play the last two measures on a

contrasting percussion instrument or found sound. For example, use hand drum and woodblocks or desk and radiator.

4. Create a melody by choosing pitches for your rhythms. Use the pitches F G A or G A B. If you use F G A, end on F. If you use G A B, end on G.

5. Play your melody on resonator bells or other pitched instrument.

Use with page 57. • Grade 5

McGraw-Hill

Don't Wait—Syncopate!

1. Clap the following rhythm, listening carefully.

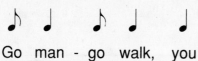

Go man - go walk, you

Now say each sentence below. Repeat each sentence as you
clap the rhythm of "Go man-go walk, you." Draw a line
through any sentences that don't fit this rhythm.

Peo-ple en-joy games.   Raise your hand and ask.

Fol-low the blue car.   Al-li-ga-tors crawl.

Create an interlude for "Mango Walk." Choose three of the
rhythm patterns below. Use one rhythm twice. Copy the
rhythms onto the four empty measures without placing the
repeated patterns next to each other. Play your interlude on
a rhythm instrument.

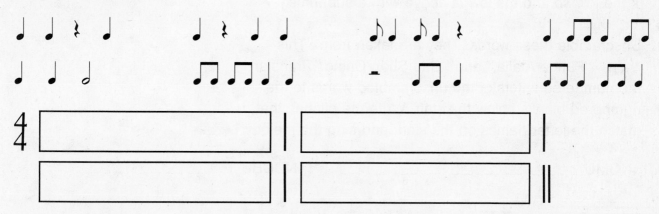

2. Look at the music below. Using the pitches F G A, fill in

the first empty measure with the syncopated rhythm

and the last empty measure with the syncopated rhythm

Sing the finished piece.

Pentatonic, Please

1. Write the pitch syllable and pitch letter name below each note. Sing each melody with pitch syllables.

Pitch syllables lower than *do* are marked with a subprime so they are not confused with higher pitches of the same letter names. (In this example, *la,* and *la* are both E.) Go back and mark the low *so* and the low *la* above with a subprime.

la, *la*

2. Unscramble these words. They are taken from "This Train," "Funga Alafia," and "Gau Shan Ching." Transfer the numbered letters of the unscrambled words to the numbered blanks below the staff. Write the pitches that match the letter names on the staff, and sing the melody.

ATINNOMU   __ __ __ __ __ __ __ __   NODBU   __ __ __ __ __
                                  6   5   1

RYLOG   __ __ __ __ __   MELCOWE   __ __ __ __ __ __ __
          3   2

TINAR   __ __ __ __ __   AGNUF   __ __ __ __ __
             4   7

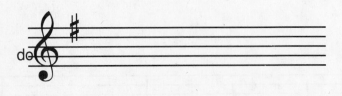

        __ __ __ __ __ __ __
         1   2   3   4   5   6   7

(See answers at the back of this book.)

Name _____

A Round of Rhythms

1. Circle each note, group of notes, or rest that gets one beat in $\frac{2}{4}$ or $\frac{4}{4}$ meter.

   a. ♫   c. 𝄾   e. ♩

   b. ♩. ♪   d. ▬   f. ♩

2. Circle each set of notes and rests that gets two beats in $\frac{2}{4}$ or $\frac{4}{4}$ meter.

   a. ♩♩   c. ♫♪♩ ♪   e. ♩ ♩

   b. 𝄾 ♩   d. 𝄾 ▬   f. ♩. ♪

3. Circle each set of notes and rests that gets four beats in $\frac{2}{4}$ or $\frac{4}{4}$ meter.

   a. ♩ 𝄾 ♫♩   c. ♩. ♫♩   e. ♩ ♩♩♩

   b. ♩ ♫♩   d. ♫ ♫   f. ♫♪ ♪ ▬

4. Complete each measure below with one of the four choices so that each measure contains four beats. Clap each completed measure.

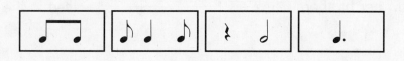

a.

b.

c.

d. (measure)

(See answers at the back of this book.)

McGraw-Hill

Name_____

Spell It Out

Read the story below. Fill in the missing letters or words by writing the letter names of the notes on the staff.

On the morning of her birthday, Juanita jumped out of  and

___ ___ ___

changed into a sweater,  jeans, and a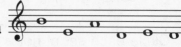

___ ___ ___ ___ ___   ___ ___ ___ ___ ___

necklace her Mom and 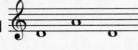 had given her. Her friends would soon

___ ___ ___

meet her at the ar  . Juanita was a video game

___ ___ ___

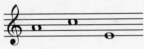 who always seemed to   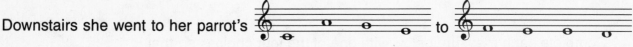 points to her high scores.

___ ___ ___   ___ ___ ___

Downstairs she went to her parrot's  to

___ ___ ___ ___ ___   ___ ___ ___ ___

him before she ate. She didn't know her brother,   , waited in the

___ ___ ___ ___

kitchen. He surprised her with a bacon-and-egg birthday breakfast

and teased her about her age.

Two words in the last sentence could also have been "spelled" on the staff. Write them below before drawing them on the staff.

___ ___ ___ ___   ___ ___ ___

(See answers at the back of this book.)

McGraw-Hill

Sweet Sixteenths (and More)

Draw a line from the rhythm to its duration.

1.   **a.** one beat

2.   **b.** two beats

3.   **c.** three beats

4.   **d.** four beats

5.   **e.** three beats

Draw the following rhythm patterns. Refer to the notes and rests drawn above. Then write the number of beats in each rhythm pattern.

6. a dotted quarter note and an eighth note   _____ beat(s)

7. four sixteenth notes, one quarter rest, one half note   _____ beat(s)

8. two sixteenths and an eighth note   _____ beat(s)

9. a quarter note tied to a quarter note, a quarter rest   _____ beat(s)

10. an eighth note, a quarter note, an eighth note, a half rest _____ beat(s)

11. two eighth notes, an eighth note and two sixteenth notes _____ beat(s)

Create your own four-beat pattern. Choose from any of the rhythms above, but make sure one of the beats contains sixteenth notes. Play your pattern for the class.

(See answers at the back of this book.)

McGraw-Hill

Check It Out

1. Which rhythm do you hear?

   a.    c.

   b.    d.

2. Which rhythm do you hear?

   a.    c.

   b.    d.

3. Which rhythm do you hear?

   a.   c.

   b.   d.

4. Choose the pitches that you hear.

   a. 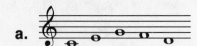   c.

   b.   d.

(See answers at the back of this book.)

Name _____

Play the Part

The Fierce Creature
A Folktale from Kenya

PEOPLE AND MATERIALS NEEDED:

Stagehand
Musicians to play each of the
following instruments:

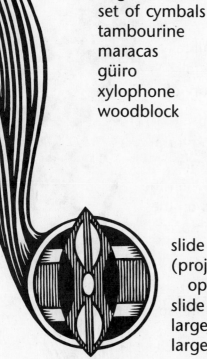

INSTRUMENTS

gong or hanging cymbal
triangle
large drum
set of cymbals
tambourine
maracas
güiro
xylophone
woodblock

CHARACTERS

Three Griots
Caterpillar
   (*Cowardly Theme:* triangle;
   Brave Theme: large drum
   and cymbals)
Hare (tambourine)
Leopard (maracas)
Rhinoceros (güiro)
Elephant (glissando up and
   down on xylophone)
Frog (woodblock)

PROPS

slide projector
(projection screen or white sheet
   optional; blank wall may be used)
slide of Africa
large, cutout Masai house
large, cutout African tree

A simple scene can be created by projecting a slide of Africa on a screen or wall. Stagehand carries in a large cutout of a Masai house, then exits. (The house should have an open doorway so the caterpillar can enter and exit when necessary.) Three griots step forward and face the audience. The sound of African drumming can be heard softly in the distance. The sounds gradually build. **[Use African rhythms on page 113.]** *Music continues. . .*

McGraw-Hill

15

1st Griot: Listen!

3rd Griot: Listen!

2nd Griot: Beating!

1st Griot: Listen!

1st and 3rd Griots: Listen!

All: Listen to the rhythm.

2nd Griot: African beat! *1st and 3rd griots join in with the rhythm, using body percussion.*

1st and 3rd Griots: Telling the folktales. . .

All: Of—Africa! *Drumming stops.*

2nd Griot *(stepping forward) [gong or hanging cymbal]:* I shall tell you a story from Eastern Africa. It was told to me by the tall Masai who live in the high country of Kenya. It is the story of "The Fierce Creature!"

1st Griot *[triangle]:* A caterpillar came crawling along, looking for a place to rest. He entered the house of the hare. *As he speaks, Cowardly Caterpillar enters from left and goes into house.* When the hare came home *[tambourine]*, he noticed strange marks on the ground in front of his house. *Hare enters from right and inspects ground in front of the house.*

Hare *(shouting) [tambourine]:* Who is in my house?

1st Griot: The Caterpillar did not want to be eaten by the Hare, so he answered in a fierce voice.

Caterpillar *(fiercely from inside the house) [large drum, ending with a cymbal crash]:* I am the terrible warrior, deadlier than the leopard. I crush the rhinoceros to earth and trample the mighty elephant.

1st Griot: The Hare was most frightened. *Hare hops about and trembles.* He didn't know what to do, so when the Leopard came padding by, searching for food, *[maracas]* the Hare stopped her. *Leopard roars off left, then enters stealthily, sniffing wind.*

Hare *[tambourine]:* There is a fierce creature in my house, Leopard. *Leopard crosses to house, sniffing stage.*

Leopard *(loudly) [maracas]:* Who is in the Hare's house?

Caterpillar *(fiercely) [large drum, ending with a cymbal crash]:* I am the terrible warrior, deadlier than the leopard. I crush the rhinoceros to earth and trample the mighty elephant. *Leopard yelps in fear and hides behind Hare.*

1st Griot: Soon a rhinoceros came charging by on his way to the water hole. *[güiro] Rhinoceros enters, snorting and charging, with his horn lowered.*

Hare *[tambourine]:* Can you help me, Rhinoceros? There is a fierce creature in my house. *Rhinoceros snorts, then charges to Hare's house.*

Rhinoceros *(loudly) [güiro]:* Who is in the Hare's house?

Caterpillar *(fiercely) [large drum, ending with a cymbal crash]:* I am the terrible warrior, deadlier than the leopard. I crush the rhinoceros to earth and trample the mighty elephant. *Rhinoceros snorts in fear and hides behind Leopard.*

1st Griot: Soon an elephant came lumbering by, looking for bananas. *[glissando on xylophone] Elephant trumpets off left, then lumbers in, pretending to look in trees.*

Hare *[tambourine]:* Can you help us, Elephant? There is a fierce creature in my house. *Elephant lumbers to the house.*

Elephant *(loudly) [glissando on xylophone]:* Who is in the Hare's house?

Caterpillar *(fiercely) [large drum, ending with a cymbal crash]:* I am the terrible warrior, deadlier than the leopard. I crush the rhinoceros to earth and trample the mighty elephant. *Elephant trumpets in fear and hides behind the rhinoceros.*

1st Griot: Finally, a clever frog came hopping by, on his way to catch bugs. *[woodblock] Frog croaks and enters left, hopping.*

Hare *[tambourine]:* Frog, can you help me? There is a fierce creature in my house. *Frog hops to house.*

Frog *[woodblock]:* Who is in the Hare's house?

Caterpillar *(fiercely) [large drum, ending with a cymbal crash]:* I am the terrible warrior, deadlier than the leopard. I crush the rhinoceros to earth and trample the mighty elephant.

Frog *(shouting) [woodblock]:* I, the hideous leaper, have come. I am slimy, green, and full of great big warts. *Caterpillar squeaks in fear and crawls out of the Hare's house and off right.*

Caterpillar *(excitedly) [triangle]:* Help! Help! *Animals watch him go, then fall down laughing.*

Frog *(bowing to the other animals) [woodblock]:* Kindly excuse me. I believe I just saw a fierce creature come crawling out of the Hare's house. I, the terrible warrior, will pursue him, for my dinner is long past due. *Frog exits right, hopping.*

Curtain

McGraw-Hill

Write the pitch syllables and letter names of the notes below.
Then sing each melody with a partner, first in pitch syllables,
then in letter names.

1. do

_____ _____ _____ _____

_____ _____ _____ _____

2. do

_____ _____ _____ _____

_____ _____ _____ _____

Fa is the fourth pitch in a major scale, and the note "C" in
the key of G. Can you identify *fa* and the rest of the pitch
syllables and letter names in the other keys below?

3. do

_____ _____ _____ _____

_____ _____ _____ _____

4. do

_____ _____ _____ _____

_____ _____ _____ _____

These excerpts from "Joyful, Joyful We Adore Thee" are
incomplete. Fill in the missing parts, whether they are notes,
pitch syllables, or letter names, and sing the completed melody.

do

mi ___ ___ *re* ___
___ C ___ A ___

___ ___ ___ *mi* ___
C ___ G B ___

(See answers at the back of this book.)

Name _____

Connecting With Copland

The famous American composer Aaron Copland (1900–1990) was born in Brooklyn, New York. As a child taking piano lessons, he showed early musical talent. He began writing his own music while still a teenager, and in 1920 his first published work appeared, a piano piece called ''The Cat and the Mouse.'' In 1921 he went to Paris for three years to study composition with Nadia Boulanger, a noted organist and teacher.

Like other composers of his time, Copland experimented with different styles and techniques. His early works were influenced by jazz and European music. Later, he used American folk-song material in his work to give it a uniquely American flavor. He was particularly successful at this in his very popular ballets *Billy the Kid* and *Rodeo*, and also *Appalachian Spring*, for which he won a Pulitzer Prize and a New York Music Critics' Circle Award.

Copland wrote several film scores and won an Academy Award in 1949 for his work on *The Heiress*. ''Fanfare for the Common Man,'' a patriotic orchestral piece he had written in 1942, is another well-known and frequently performed favorite of Americans.

Although Copland wrote a considerable amount of music throughout his lifetime, his musical career was not limited to composing. He taught, conducted, wrote a number of books on music, and lectured extensively. In 1964 Copland was given the Presidential Medal of Freedom for his contribution to American artistic life.

1. Where did Copland study for three years?
2. What type of music did Copland use in his compositions to give them an American flavor?
3. Name Copland's very popular ballets.

(See answers at the back of this book.)

Use with pages 134 and 216. • Grade 5

Step Right Up!

A dotted half note (♩.) gets three beats. Circle any dotted half notes in the example below. A whole note (o) gets four beats. Draw an X on the measure that has a whole note. A whole rest (–) means four beats of silence. Box the measure that has a whole rest.

Work with a partner. One person pats the beat. The other person pats the rhythm.

Draw a line from the staff to the matching set of pitch syllables. Remember: When a syllable such as *ti* is written with a subprime, that note is lower than *do*.

1.

a. *fa mi re mi do*

2.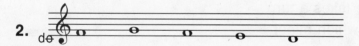

b. *do ti₁ do mi so*

3.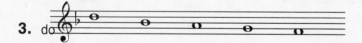

c. *fa so fa mi re*

4.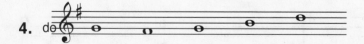

d. *la fa mi re do*

(See answers at the back of this book.)

Name

Foil the Phantom

The Phantom, who only listens to music in a minor key, has trapped you and your classmates in the basement. Before he will even consider releasing you, you must sing for him. Echo the following minor patterns after you hear them. Use your very best voice!

Next, choose eight people from your class who will each choose a pattern to play. As each classmate takes a turn playing, the rest of the class should decide which minor pattern was heard.

Now write your own minor melody. Be sure to start and end on *la*₁.

With the class, trade melodies to play and sing.

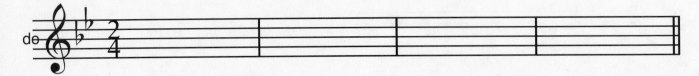

McGraw-Hill

Name _____

Check It Out

1. What do you hear?

   a. changed   **b.** unchanged voices

2. What do you hear?

   a. changed   **b.** unchanged voices

3. What do you hear?

   a. changed   **b.** unchanged voices

4. Which of these is major?

   a. Example A   **b.** Example B   **c.** Example C

5. Which of these is minor?

   a. Example A   **b.** Example B   **c.** Example C

(See answers at the back of this book.)

Focus on a Freedom Fighter: Harriet Tubman

Araminta (nicknamed "Harriet") Ross (ca. 1821–1913) was born in Maryland. Her parents were enslaved African Americans on the plantation of Edward Brodas. The sixth of eleven children, Harriet lived in a one-room cabin with a dirt floor and no furniture. At six, Harriet was put to work as a maid and took care of children. When she was twelve, she started working in the fields. She also hauled wood and split rails.

In 1844, Harriet married John Tubman, a free man. Five years later, she was warned by another slave that she was about to be sold. She left her family and escaped to freedom. Along the way, she was aided by the "Underground Railroad," the network of people who helped enslaved people escape.

Once she had gained her own freedom, Harriet joined the Underground Railroad and became a "conductor," a person who helped transport people to freedom. By the time Harriet performed her last rescue in November of 1860, she had led nearly 300 people to freedom. She was given the title "Moses," because Moses had led the captive Israelites out of Egypt and to freedom.

Although she never learned to read or write, Harriet found a way to devote much of the rest of her life to helping others. During the Civil War, she served as a nurse and spy for the Union. Years later, she opened a home for elderly African Americans and helped promote the rights of African American women. Of all of her accomplishments, Harriet Tubman was most proud of her work on the Underground Railroad. She said, "I never ran my train off the track and I never lost a passenger."

1. What made Harriet decide to escape?
2. What did a conductor on the Underground Railroad do?
3. Why do you think Harriet risked her life to save others?

McGraw-Hill

(See answers at the back of this book.)

Opera Over Easy

On pages 144-147 of your book, you read about the opera *Harriet, the Woman Called Moses*, by Thea Musgrave. Although every opera is different in story, characters, sets, and music, they still have many elements in common.

Operas are plays set to music. An opera composer works with a libretto to write the score. The libretto is the text that the singers perform, and it may be written by a librettist or the composer. For some operas, the librettist takes the story from a play, a novel, or historical events. For others, the librettist and the composer work together to create the story.

The score of the opera is the music the composer writes for the orchestra and singers. Both of these parts work together to tell the opera's story in a very dramatic way.

An opera company is made up of many musicians, both singers and instrumentalists, who play in the orchestra. The orchestra plays throughout the opera, sometimes with singers and sometimes without them. Besides helping to move the action along through their music, they also have another important role at the beginning of the opera. They play an introduction called an overture.

Singers may perform in a chorus (a large group of singers who sometimes comment on the action), as soloists, or as part of a duet. A soloist may sing an aria, which is an expressive song for one person. Two characters who sing together perform a duet (a song for two people). Sometimes characters can also sing in a speech-like type of singing called recitative.

Soloists are usually main characters in the opera, and they can have one of six different types of voices. Women's voices range from soprano (the highest) to alto (the lowest) with a mezzo-soprano in between. The highest voice for a man is the tenor, followed by the baritone, which is in the middle range, and the bass, which is the lowest type of male voice. Every singer, despite the type of voice he or she has, must have a voice that can be heard throughout the auditorium. Unlike popular artists that you know, opera singers do not usually use microphones.

McGraw-Hill

Are you an expert on opera? Work this crossword to find out.

ACROSS

2. Large group of singers
3. Music to an opera
4. Play set to music
7. Melody for a soloist
8. Male voice between bass and tenor
13. Opera text
14. Lowest man's voice
15. Highest type of woman's voice
17. Scottish female composer and conductor
18. "Hickory, dickory, dock, ____ ____ ran up the clock."

DOWN

1. *Harriet, the Woman Called* ____
3. Type of African American songs that "Go Down, Moses" and "This Train" are
4. Introduction to an opera
5. Main character in Thea Musgrave's opera
6. Song for two people
9. Speech-like type of song
10. Type of female voice between soprano and alto: ____-soprano
11. Highest male voice
12. Person who writes opera text
16. Lowest woman's voice

(See answers at the back of this book.)

Name

Accompanying "America, the Beautiful"

Play this music to "America, the Beautiful" on a C instrument
while your class sings.

McGraw-Hill

Page 2

Play this music to "America, the Beautiful" on a B♭ instrument while your class sings.

Play this music to "America, the Beautiful" on an E♭ instrument
while your class sings.

Name _____

A Key to Signatures

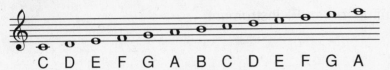

C D E F G A B C D E F G A

All flat key signatures except F major (the key of one flat) are named by the letter name of the next to the last flat in the key. Sharp key signatures are named by the letter name one line or space up from the name of the key's last sharp.

1. Name the four key signatures below. Choose from B♭ major, C major, D major, F major, and G major.

    a.   **b.**   **c.**   **d.**   **e.**

    _____   _____   _____   _____   _____

2. In this key of _____, circle all the flatted notes. Play the melody.

3. In this key of _____, circle all the sharped notes. Play the melody.

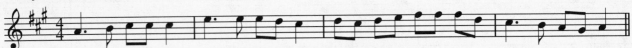

4. Look for the accidentals in the example below. Write "F" above the flats, "S" above the sharps, and "N" above the naturals. Play the melody.

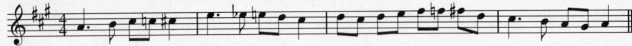

5. Change these scales by drawing sharps or flats before the correct notes. Refer to the key signatures above if you need help.

    a. D major   **b.** B♭ major

   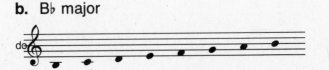

(See answers at the back of this book.)

Composing in C

Write a melody in $\frac{2}{4}$.

First, choose your rhythms. Use any of the rhythms below just once, or repeat them. Keep in mind that repeating a pattern can help to balance a piece of music.

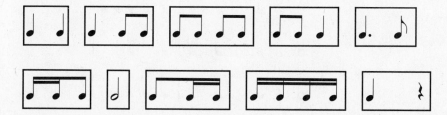

Next, choose the pitches. Use any or all of the notes in the C major scale, given below. Start and end your melody on *do*.

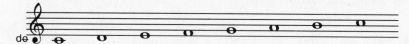

Your melody can either move stepwise (from one note to the next) or by leaps (skipping notes). Play or sing your finished melody and share it with the class.

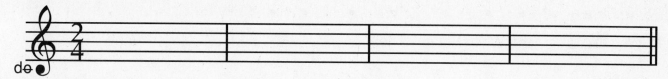

Now work with a partner to combine two melodies into an eight-measure piece. Write it below. You can use one melody as the beginning and the other as the end, or alternate measures of each. Perform your eight-measure melody for the class.

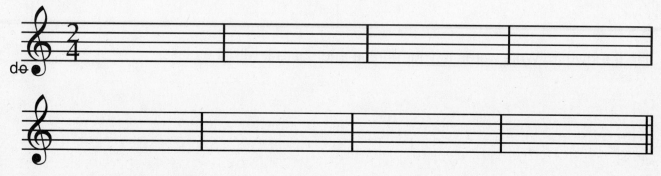

Take Your Time Signature

Match these phrases from "Down the River," "Pat Works on the Railway," and "Row, Row, Row Your Boat" with their rhythms.

1. Down the riv-er, oh down the riv-er, oh

2. Row, row, row your boat

3. Fil-li-me-oo-re-i-re-ay

4. Life is but a dream.

Answer questions 5 and 6 by writing the words in the blanks under the rhythm. Clap and chant both exercises when you have finished.

5. Name the last three months of the year. ___ - ___ - ___, ___ - ___ - ___, ___ - ___ - ___.

6. Who lives in the White House? The ___ - ___ - ___.

7. Create your own four-beat rhythmic phrase. Choose two of the following patterns, or repeat one pattern.

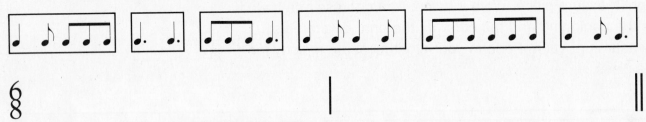

Clap the rhythm. Write words to your phrase and share it with the class.

(See answers at the back of this book.)

McGraw-Hill

$\frac{2}{4}$, $\frac{6}{8}$: Can You Tell the Difference, Mate?

$\frac{2}{4}$ meter and $\frac{6}{8}$ meter are similar because both have two beats in each measure. They are different, though, because the beats in $\frac{2}{4}$ ($\frac{2}{♩}$) time are broken into two parts, while the beats in $\frac{6}{8}$ ($\frac{2}{♩.}$) time are broken into three parts. Say and clap each example to hear and feel the difference.

1.

This   is   in   two - four.   Do   you   need   to   hear   some   more?
Beats: 1   2   1   2   1   2   1   2

2.

This   is   a   pat-tern   in   six - eight.   How man-y   parts   are   in   each   beat?
Beats: 1   2   1   2   1   2   1   2

Fill in the unfinished measures by drawing a note, a rest, or sets of notes and rests. Choose from the notes and rests below. Use each choice only once. Clap or play your completed measures.

3. $\frac{6}{8}$

4. $\frac{2}{4}$

Clap these four-beat rhythms. Add the meter signature ($\frac{2}{4}$ or $\frac{6}{8}$) and bar lines. (Look at examples 1 and 2 to see how they are done.)

5.

6.

7.

8.

9.

10.

(See answers at the back of this book.)

McGraw-Hill

Name _____

Minor Adjustments

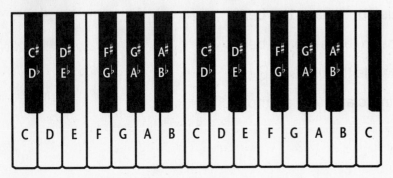

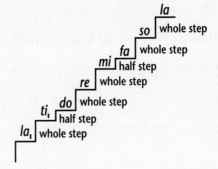

Recall that minor scales begin and end on *la*, while major scales begin and end on *do*. Refer to the keyboard and stair steps to fill in the blanks.

Fill in the missing notes, pitch syllables, or letter names. Are these scales major or minor? Name and play them.

1. Name: _____

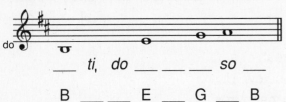

____ *ti,* *do* ____ ____ ____ *so* ____

B ____ ____ E ____ G ____ B

2. Name: _____

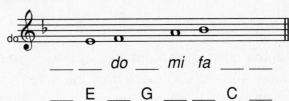

____ ____ *do* ____ *mi* *fa* ____ ____

____ E ____ G ____ ____ C ____

Write the pitch letter names and pitch syllables of each note. Then identify these scales by letter name and "major" or "minor." Sing the scales using pitch syllables.

3. Name: _____

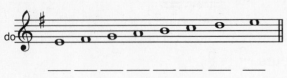

____ ____ ____ ____ ____ ____ ____ ____

____ ____ ____ ____ ____ ____ ____ ____

4. Name: _____

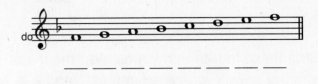

____ ____ ____ ____ ____ ____ ____ ____

____ ____ ____ ____ ____ ____ ____ ____

5. Write a G minor scale. Play it.

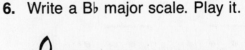

6. Write a B♭ major scale. Play it.

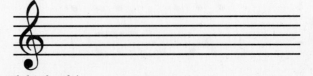

(See answers at the back of this book.)

Use with page 192. • Grade 5

McGraw-Hill

Name

Name _____

Spell and Seek

Number the words made only of letters from A to G. Then copy them under the staves provided before "spelling" them on the staff. You should discover 18 words like this.

ACCOMPANIMENT	DEED	KEY SIGNATURE
ADAGE	*DO RE MI*	LET'S GET GOING!
AMERICA	DOTTED HALF NOTE	MAJOR
ARIA	DOTTED QUARTER NOTE	MANGO WALK
BAD	DOTTED QUARTER REST	MELODY
BADGE	EIGHTH NOTE	MINOR
BAG	EIGHTH REST	OPERA
BAGGAGE	FACE	OVERTURE
BEAD	FADE	PENTATONIC
BEE	FED	QUARTER NOTE
BEEF	FEE	QUARTER REST
BEG	FIERCE CREATURE	RHYTHM
CAB	FLAT	SHARP
CABBAGE	HALF NOTE	SIXTEENTH NOTE
CAFE	HALF REST	SYNCOPATION
COPLAND	HARRIET TUBMAN	WHOLE NOTE
DEAF	JOYFUL, JOYFUL	WHOLE REST

1. _____   2. _____   3. _____

4. _____   5. _____   6. _____

(See answers at the back of this book.)

Name _____

RESOURCE MASTER 4•7

Page 2

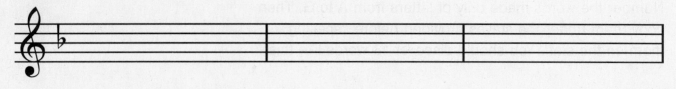

7. _____   8. _____   9. _____

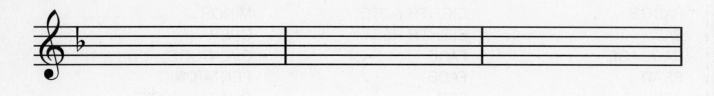

10. _____   11. _____   12. _____

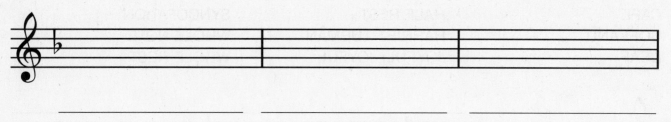

13. _____   14. _____   15. _____

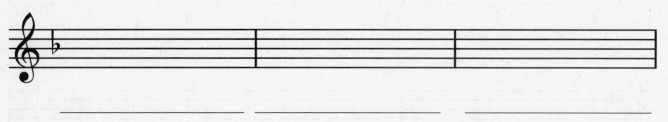

16. _____   17. _____   18. _____

(See answers at the back of this book.)

19. _____   20. _____

Think of two more words made of letters from A to G and "spell" them on the staff above. Play each "word."

All of the words listed on the first page of "Spell and Seek" are hidden in this puzzle. Look for them spelled forwards, backwards, from top to bottom, bottom to top, or diagonally. How quickly can you find all of them? One word has been circled for you already.

```
D O T T E D Q U A R T E R N O T E Y E T O N H T H G I E
M E L K S E T R O N I M L Z S A C P H V P B C W A B A T
F A C E P A F N B A C O B A D S E J E L A T H Y L U R O
Q O N I E V K H F M F X N R O N T R Y G E O B L F T X N
U U P G T A J V C B Y I E P T S T M O Z L T L E R M I R
A E E H O L I L E U W R E A E U Y D E E R A U T E N V E
R J S T N W P R X T U R T R R X E N R L C K F S S I R T
T G L H E C A M A T A O R E C G P E C C O G B G T W P R
E O M R L D O L A E N E L O D E S N O O W D V E Y L I A
R W K E O Z F N K I T R X A E T C M G V P H Y T A O H U
R E P S H C G D C R M H B Y K T P R U R C A S G E D C Q
E H C T W I A W A R C B C W G A O H E K L R T O E W A K
S F G T S C B U M A P E K O N F B N S A Z P J I M M I F
T E O Y I U Q I B H G E R I P C X A F V T D H N O C M D
B W E R C D P B S A B F M H A L Q E G L S U C G P N E R
C K E L E O A H D L R E H F Y T A U C G A T R W Q C R E
F M H T A G U A N O N Z E X E T O N F L A H D E T T O D
A S T N E N C F V T A S T R M I H E D S P G S U I A D E
E O V S J O Y F U L J O Y F U L B M A J O R E M C X E F
D E E D S I X T E E N T H N O T E D A F L E W P R A H S
```

(See answers at the back of this book.)

Eight Times Two

Write your own eight-beat rhythmic accompaniment to "Et tan' patate là cuite." Choose two of the four patterns below and decide the order in which they'll be played. Copy them into the measures provided.

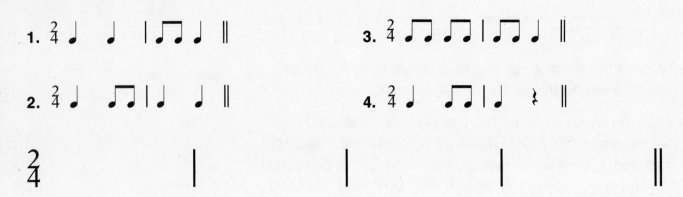

Play your accompaniment through six times so it will last throughout the entire song as your class sings "Et tan' patate là cuite."

"Pat Works on the Railway" is in 6/8 time. Choose two patterns from among the following to create an eight-beat rhythmic accompaniment for this song. Decide the order in which they'll be played and copy them into the measures below.

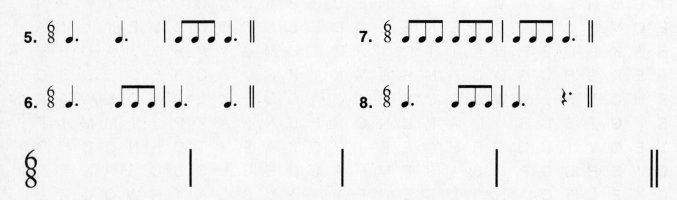

Play your accompaniment through four times to accompany your classmates while they sing a verse of "Pat Works on the Railway."

Name _____

Check It Out

1. Choose the meter you hear.

   a. $\frac{4}{4}$ **b.** $\frac{6}{8}$

2. Which of the following examples shows what you hear?

   a.    **b.**

3. Which of the following examples shows what you hear?

   a.    **b.**

4. Choose the $\frac{6}{8}$ pattern you hear.

   a.    **c.**

   b.    **d.**

5. Which pattern is in $\frac{6}{8}$ meter?

   a. Example A   **b.** Example B

6. Which pattern is in $\frac{6}{8}$ meter?

   a. Example A   **b.** Example B

7. Which pattern is in $\frac{6}{8}$ meter?

   a. Example A   **b.** Example B

(See answers at the back of this book.)

RESOURCE MASTER 4•10 Pattern

Covering $\frac{4}{4}$

Cut out the ten pieces of the quilt below. Each square equals
one beat. Arrange your pieces into rows of four beats. Next,
decide on the order in which you want them to fit together. By
organizing your patches, you will create a sixteen-beat quilt.
Clap or play it with a rhythm instrument.

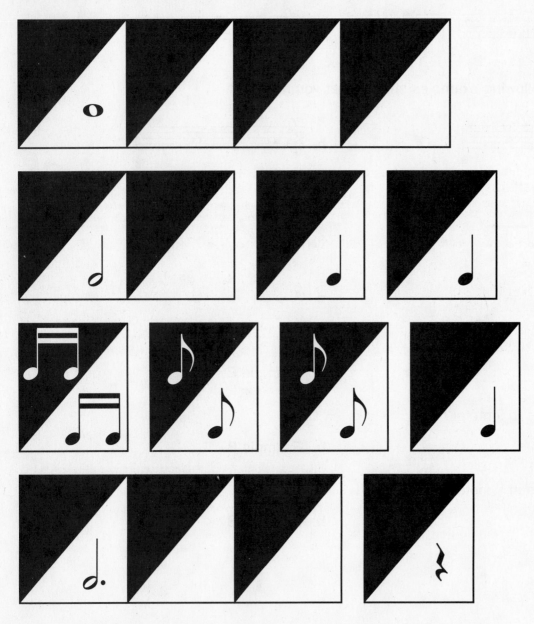

Rearrange your pieces into new four-beat patterns to create
a different rhythmic quilt. Clap or play it. How many quilts can
you make this way?

(See answers at the back of this book.)

Name _____

All in a Chord

Many songs can be harmonized with only two chords: the I chord, built on the first step of the scale, *do*, and the V chord, built on the fifth step of the scale, *so*. With your finger, trace the C major scale on the keyboard below before filling in the blanks with the correct letter names.

1. In the key of C major, the I chord is built on the pitch _____ .

2. In the key of C major, the V chord is built on the

    pitch _____ .

The I chord is made up of *do*, *mi*, and *so* (the first, third, and fifth pitches of a scale). The V chord is made up of *so*, *ti*, and *re*ˡ (the fifth, seventh, and second steps of a scale). Look at the keyboard again. On the staff below, circle the notes of the I chord in C major. Then box the notes of the V chord.

3.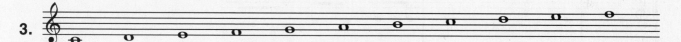

One way to write a chord on the staff is in "root position."

*   Write the root of the chord (*do* in the I chord, *so* in the V chord) first.
*   Stack the other pitches in the chord directly above the root.
*   Play all of the pitches in the chord at the same time.

4.

A chord can be labeled by the letter name of its root. Write in the letter names of the I and V chords. Then play each chord.

(See answers at the back of this book.)

RESOURCE MASTER 5•1

Page 2

Now that you know the I and V chords in C major, you can accompany songs. Look at "Good News," below, and notice the chord symbols "C" and "G" above the melody. Write the chords on the staff below in half notes. (Two measures have been done for you.)

While some of your classmates sing "Good News," play the accompaniment on guitar, autoharp, keyboard, resonator bells, or an Orff instrument.

(See answers at the back of this book.)

Intrada für Pauken, Trompeten, und Flöten
by Gunild Keetman

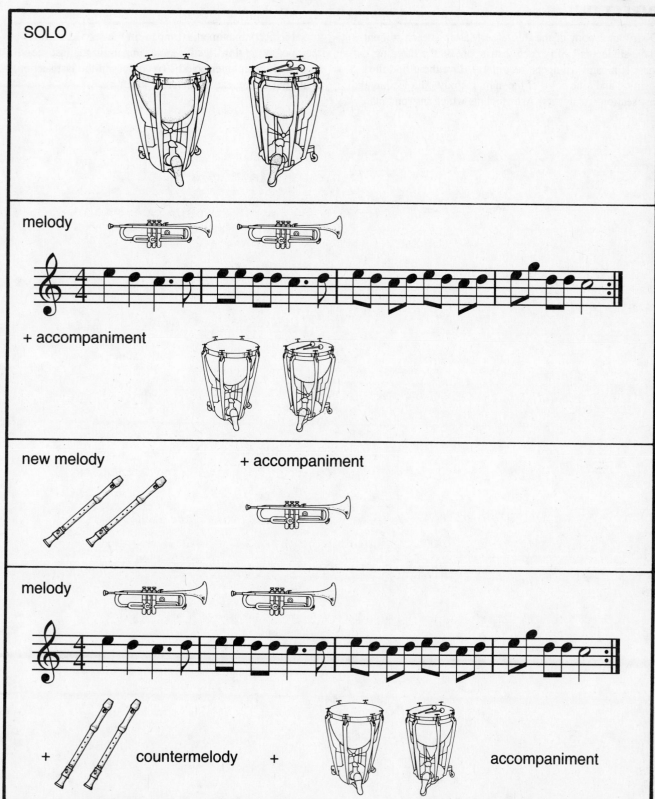

USING RESOURCE MASTER 5•2

DIRECTIONS:

Distribute a copy of the Resource Master to each student. Have students identify each instrument on the listening map. (timpani, trumpets, recorders) Have them find the location and tone color of the main melody. (the second and last sections; trumpets) Ask students which instruments play the accompaniment, (timpani in the second section, trumpet in the third section, and timpani in the last section) and the countermelody. (recorders in the last section) Point out the repeat signs before listening.

Introducing "Intrada"

Listen to "Intrada" by Gunild Keetman. Notice that the introduction is a 24-measure timpani solo on the pitches C and G_1. Using your own combination of the rhythms ♩, ♬♬, ♩., ♪♫, ♬♫, ♫♬ and 𝄽 , write a new introduction to the piece. If you are using pitches, write letter names below the rhythms. Keep in mind that the piece has a strong marching tempo, so your rhythm should keep moving.

$$\frac{4}{4}$$

Perform your introduction on timpani, on unpitched rhythm instruments, or with body percussion. To make it the right length, play it six times. You may also combine your four-measure segment with those of two classmates as follows:

- One person plays his or her segment.
- The group echoes each measure immediately after hearing it. This makes each segment eight measures long.
- The next person plays his or her segment and the group echoes. Begin each segment without a break in the rhythm.

Use body percussion or rhythm instruments to create another piece. Use the rhythms below.

- Start from any *outside* block.
- "Write" a measure by playing four blocks of rhythms. Move horizontally, vertically, or if you begin from a corner box, diagonally.
- To use this as an introduction to "Intrada," play 24 measures.

RESOURCE MASTER 5•4 Practice

"Trampin'" from I to V

Look at the notation below. It is in F major. Remember that a
I chord is made up of *do*, *mi*, and *so*. A V chord is made up
of *so*, *ti*, and *re*. Circle the pitches that are part of the I chord.
Box the pitches that are part of the V chord.

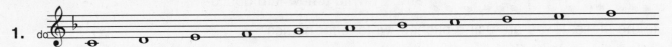

1.

2. On which pitch is the I chord built in F major? ____
   On which pitch is the V chord built? ____

Here is the refrain from "Trampin'."

3. Create an accompaniment for this song. Write the chords
   shown above the staff. Use the following rhythmic pattern:

Take turns singing "Trampin' " and playing its
accompaniment on autoharp, keyboard, guitar, resonator
bells, or an Orff instrument. You can play the accompaniment
for the refrain only or play it twice to accompany the entire
song.

(See answers at the back of this book.)

McGraw-Hill

Playing With Rhythms

1. Write a four-beat rhythm pattern to accompany "La bamba" and "Ezekiel Saw de Wheel." Combine the rhythms ♩, ♫♫, and ♩ Use body percussion to perform your pattern.

$\frac{2}{4}$ | ‖

Rhythm:

Body Percussion:

Perform your pattern eight times to accompany "Ezekiel Saw de Wheel," and four times for the refrain of "La bamba."

2. Play rhythm bingo. Fill in the empty boxes in the card below with notes and rests. Choose from these rhythms:

	B	I	N	G	O	
1						
2						
3						
4						
5						
	B	I	N	G	O	

Listen as your teacher calls B, I, N, G, or O and a number from 1 to 5. Find that block on your card. If your teacher calls the note or rest you wrote in that square, mark the square in pencil. The winner is the first person to match all the blocks in a row or column (horizontally, diagonally, or vertically) with the notes or rests the teacher calls.

RESOURCE MASTER 5•6 Practice

Color My Song

Striking many different parts of a drum is one way to produce different types of tone colors. When the head of a drum is hit, you will hear a rounder and deeper tone than when its side or rim is struck.

Another way to experiment with a drum's tone colors is to vary the objects used to strike the drum. Listen carefully as you tap a drum with a drumstick, the tips of your fingers, your nails, your knuckles, or the palm of your hand.

Now try patting your desk, stamping your foot, and clapping. Each of the sounds you've made has a particular tone color. After experimenting with several different tone colors, choose three that you'd like to use to accompany "Arirang."

1. Pick four rhythm boxes below, making sure that one of the three-beat patterns is repeated. Cut them out and arrange them within the four empty measures.

2. Decide which tone color will be used for each note and label the beats.

3. Play the rhythm pattern four times to accompany "Arirang."

Take turns singing "Arirang." Share your arrangement with the class.

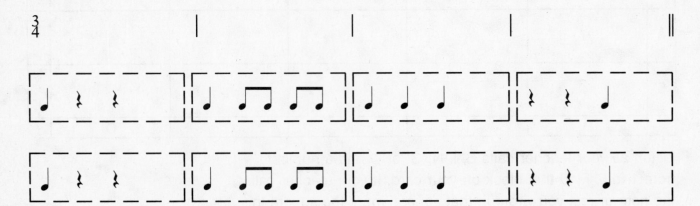

Check It Out

1. Which meter do you hear?

   a. $\frac{3}{4}$ b. $\frac{4}{4}$ c. $\frac{6}{8}$

2. Which meter do you hear?

   a. $\frac{3}{4}$ b. $\frac{4}{4}$ c. $\frac{6}{8}$

3. Which meter do you hear?

   a. $\frac{3}{4}$ b. $\frac{4}{4}$ c. $\frac{6}{8}$

4. Choose the pattern you hear.

5. Choose the pattern you hear.

6. Choose the pattern you hear.

7. Which chord progression do you hear?

   a. I I V I   **b.** I V I V   **c.** I V V I   **d.** I I I V

(See answers at the back of this book.)

String Quartet Op. 33, No. 3, Fourth Movement
by Franz Joseph Haydn

Aa Theme

A
a 4 bars
4 bars
b 6 bars
8 bars
c 4 bars
4 bars
6 bars
(minor)

B
14 bars
4 bars
8 bars
8 bars

A'
a 4 bars
4 bars
b 6 bars
7 bars
c 4 bars
4 bars
6 bars
(minor)

C
8 bars
10 bars

A''
a 4 bars
4 bars
8 bars
b 6 bars

Coda
10 bars
14 bars

USING RESOURCE MASTER 6•1

DIRECTIONS:

Distribute a copy of the Resource Master to each student. Point out the rhythm of the theme and echo-clap the rhythm. Have the students find each lettered section and subsection on the map, and tell the form. (A B A¹ C A" coda) The number of measures for each part is given to help keep track of elapsed time. The map shows texture, relative pitch levels, and dynamics in an abstract way.

Darker dots represent louder sounds. The downward-flowing ribbons represent descending runs, and the curled symbols represent ornamented passages. Point out the quarter rests, the fermata, and the parts labeled minor. Also note the repeat signs before listening. You may wish to have the students color the A sections one color and the B, C, and coda sections contrasting colors.

Rhythmatics

Play RHYTHMATICS. Cut out the spinner and arrow along the dotted lines and back them with cardboard. Attach the arrow to the spinner with a fastener. Cut out the markers and use them to move around the gameboard.

Two or more players begin on "Student Musician" and use the spinner to determine the note value they must move ahead. (Neither of the black triangles should be used as moving spaces.) Each triangle on the board is a sixteenth note; each square is an eighth note. Spinning the quarter rest means the player loses a turn. Spinning the repeat marks means the player does not move until he/she spins again. Players must follow the directions of any box they land in. The first person to become a "Conductor" wins.

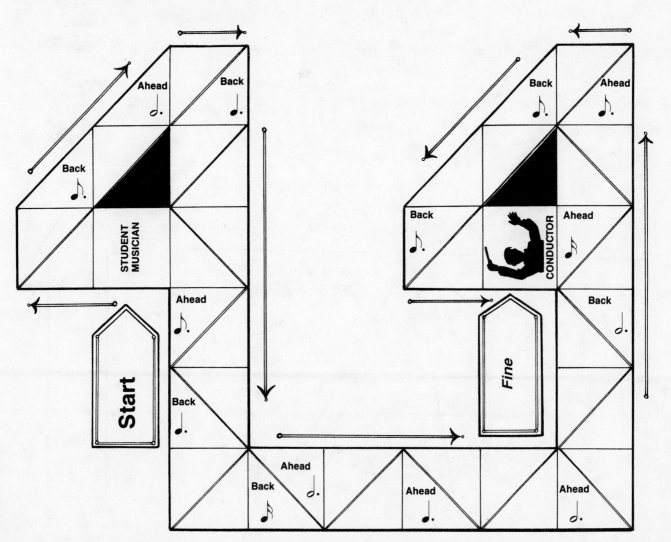

Page 2

Use this chart to remind you of note values.

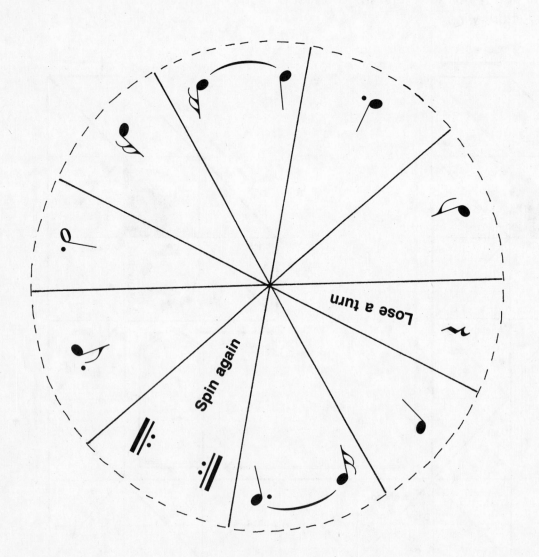

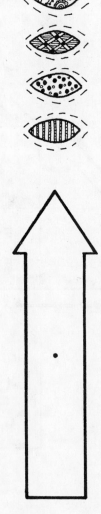

Create a Canon

Learn this melody and sing it with pitch syllables.

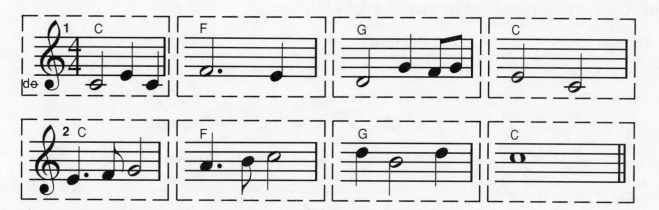

The numbers 1 and 2 indicate the melody is a two-part canon. To sing the canon, form two groups. Group 1 sings from 1. When they reach 2, Group 2 should start singing at 1.

Both parts work together because the measures that coincide are built on pitches from the same chords. Measures 1 and 5, as well as 4 and 8, are built on the C chord (C E G); measures 2 and 6 are built on the F chord (F A C); measures 3 and 7 are built on the G chord (G B D).

You can use this melody as a model for composing your own canon. Replace each measure of the original melody with a melodic segment you've written. Use notes from the chords on the first and third beats of each measure, following the chord pattern (C F G C, C F G C). Avoid large leaps so your melody will be easy to sing. In two groups, try out your canon. You may write words or use instruments.

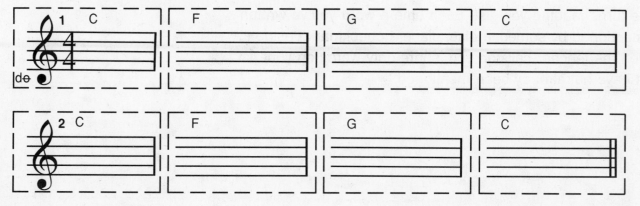

McGraw-Hill

Name _____

A Word About Wind Quintet

As you listen to "Suite for Wind Quintet," First Movement, by
Ruth Crawford-Seeger, list words that describe each section.

A Section

_____

_____

_____

_____

_____

_____

_____

_____

_____

_____

_____

B Section

_____

_____

_____

_____

_____

_____

_____

_____

_____

_____

_____

A Section

_____

_____

_____

_____

_____

_____

_____

_____

_____

_____

_____

Take turns reading your list. Each time a word you've written
is mentioned by someone else, place a checkmark beside it.
When the teacher calls on you, share only words on your list
that have not already been mentioned.

Name _____

Suite for Wind Quintet, First Movement
by Ruth Crawford-Seeger

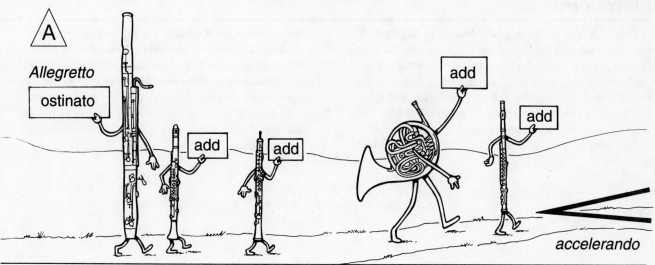

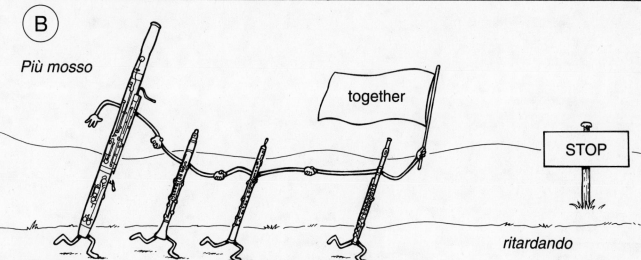

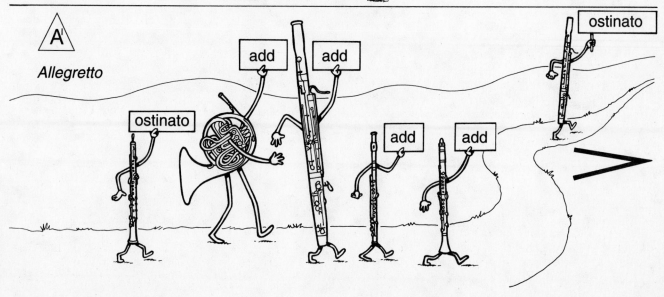

USING RESOURCE MASTER 6·5

DIRECTIONS:

Distribute a copy of the Resource Master to each student. Have students find the three lettered sections on the map. (A B A'). Have the students identify each instrument on the listening map. (bassoon, clarinet, oboe, French horn, flute in the A section; bassoon, clarinet, oboe, and flute in the B section; oboe, French horn, bassoon, flute, and clarinet in the A' section) Have students look at the way the instruments are moving and tell what they think will be different about the B section. (It will be faster) Help them to find the tempo markings and understand their meanings. (*allegretto:* moderately fast, *accelerando:* getting faster, *più mosso:* more motion, *ritardando:* getting slower, stop, *allegretto*) Be sure that students note the ostinato signs, one in the A section, two in the A' section. Point out the crescendo sign in the A section, and the decrescendo in the A' section.

A B A My Way

Plan a piece in A B A form based on "Suite for Wind Quintet," First Movement, by Ruth Crawford-Seeger. Choose your favorite descriptive words from the list you created on Resource Master 6•4, or use other descriptive words.

A	B	A
_____	_____	_____

Use the work sheet below to help you plan your composition. Remember that the B section should contrast with the A section in some way. Include changes in tempo based on what you heard in the "Suite for Wind Quintet."

	A	B	A
Dynamics			
Tone Color			
Meter			
Pitches			
Style			
Mood			

Invite a composer to your classroom and discuss your ideas. Find out how the composer plans a composition.

RESOURCE MASTER 6•7 Practice

Harmony IV All

The IV chord, built on the fourth step of the scale, is used to harmonize many songs. It includes the fourth, sixth, and eighth (or first) pitches of a major scale (*fa*, *la*, and *do*). Here is the IV chord in the key of C.

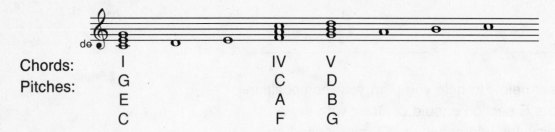

Chords: I   IV   V

Pitches: G   C   D
           E   A   B
           C   F   G

Now write the I, IV, and V chords in the keys of F major and G major. Name the pitch each IV chord is built on and list all the notes in each chord.

In the key of F, the IV chord is built on __ .   In the key of G, the IV chord is built on __ .

Chords: I   IV   V   Chords: I   IV   V

Pitches: _____ _____ _____   Pitches: _____ _____ _____

         _____ _____ _____   _____ _____ _____

         _____ _____ _____   _____ _____ _____

Knowing the I, IV, and V chords in three keys will help you harmonize many songs. Sometimes you may want to contrast the accompaniments for the verse and the chorus of a song by using different rhythm patterns for each.

Sing "Li'l 'Liza Jane" from your book. This song is in the key of C and in $\frac{2}{4}$ time. Because of its melodic rhythm, a pattern of quarter notes, eighth notes, and half notes would work well for its accompaniment. Follow the chord symbols above the music.

(See answers at the back of this book.)

Name_____

Copy your accompaniment onto the blank staves below. You
may write your own rhythm pattern or use the following:

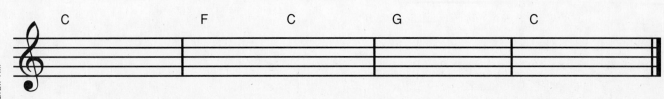

(See answers at the back of this book.)

McGraw-Hill

Page 3

Find "Down the River" in your book. Because this song has a rolling $\frac{6}{8}$ rhythm, an accompaniment pattern might include combinations of ♩ ♪♩ ♪, ♫♫ ♩., ♩. ♩., or ♩.

Sing "Down the River" to decide which rhythms you prefer. Write an accompaniment to the refrain below. Follow the chords indicated above the music.

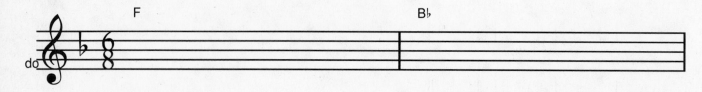

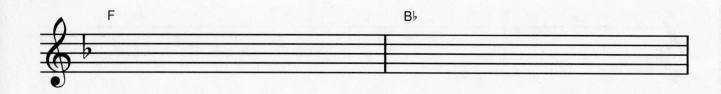

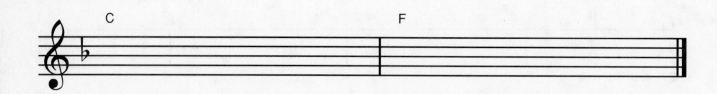

(See answers at the back of this book.)

McGraw-Hill

How Blue are You?

Develop your own twelve-bar blues lyrics to the tune of
"Good Mornin' Blues." First, list some reasons a person
might feel blue.

_____   _____

_____   _____

Next, review the lyrics and rhythms below. Remember the
rhyme scheme for twelve-bar blues: one line repeats and a
third line rhymes with the first two.

Write your own twelve-bar blues lyrics below. Match the
syllables of your words to the rhythm patterns.

Sample: My friend is gone, _   moved a - way last night. _   My

New lyrics: _____

Sample: friend   is gone, _   moved a - way last night. _   I'm

New lyrics: _____

Sample: feel - in' so blue, _   oh when will   I feel   right?

New lyrics: _____

Plan a performance with your friends. Play "Good Mornin',
Blues" and sing the original first verse. Now sing your new
lyrics for the second verse. Play the song again as two more
of your classmates take turns singing their lyrics for the third
and fourth verses. Join your friends in playing and singing
the first verse again.

The Answer Is...

Work with a partner to play this question and answer game.
Clap the first two-measure rhythm while your partner answers
with a new rhythm pattern that uses [♪♩♪] at least
once. Write the answer pattern in the space provided. Trade
roles for each question.

QUESTIONS   **ANSWERS**

1.

2.

3.

4.

You have created four four-measure phrases. Take turns
clapping each of these to become familiar with them.

Now choose any one of the phrases to clap. Your partner
must echo the phrase but change one beat into a rest or a
different rhythm. You must recognize the change and tell
your partner what it is. To keep score, give yourself a point
each time you correctly identify a rhythmic change. Subtract
a point each time you don't.

Switch roles after each four-measure question. The winner is
the person with the most points after all the phrases have
been played.

Name

Matchmaker

1. Back the cards below with thin cardboard, then cut them out.

2. Shuffle the cards and lay them face down in rows on a desk or table.

3. Select the order in which players will take their turns.

4. Each player takes a turn by completely flipping over two cards so everyone can see them. If the cards match (each descriptive card corresponds to a symbol card), the player places them in his/her discard pile and selects two more cards. If the cards do not match, they are placed face down again and the next player takes a turn.

5. Pay attention to other players' turns too. Your strategy should be to remember the positions of as many of the turned-over cards as possible.

6. After all the cards have been collected, the player with the most matches wins.

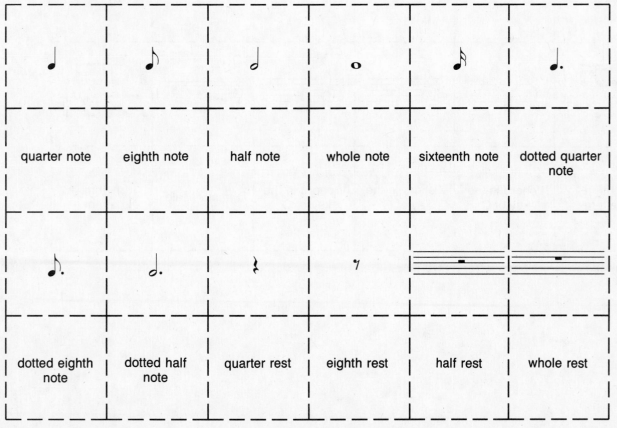

(See answers at the back of this book.)

McGraw-Hill

p	*pp*	*f*	*ff*	*mp*	*mf*
soft (piano)	very soft (pianissimo)	loud (forte)	very loud (fortissimo)	medium soft (mezzo piano)	medium loud (mezzo forte)
C major	G major	F major	D major	B♭ major	syncopated rhythm
$\frac{2}{4}$ rhythm pattern	I chord in the key of C	V chord in the key of G	IV chord in the key of C	D minor scale	$\frac{6}{8}$ rhythm pattern

1. Choose the form that you hear.

   a. A B A   **b.** A B A C A   **c.** A B   **d.** A A B A

2. Choose the form that you hear.

   a. A B A C A   **b.** A B   **c.** A B A   **d.** A B C

3. Choose the form that you hear.

   a. A B   **b.** A B A   **c.** A A B A   **d.** A B A C A

4. Which chord progression do you hear?

   a. I IV V I   **b.** I V IV I   **c.** I IV I V   **d.** I I IV V

5. Which chord progression do you hear?

   a. I V IV V   **b.** I IV IV I   **c.** I IV V I   **d.** I V IV I

(See answers at the back of this book.)

RESOURCE MASTER C•1 *Speech Piece*

Fifty Nifty Fun

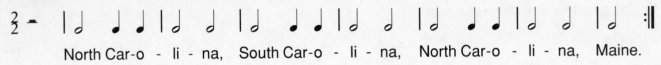

North Car-o - li - na, South Car-o - li - na, North Car-o - li - na, Maine.

North   Car - o - li - na,   South Car - o - li - na,   Maine.

North   Car - o - li   -   na,   Maine.

New   York,   Ver - mont, and   North Car - o - li - na,   Maine.

New York, New York, New York, New York, Lou - i - si - an - a, Ver - mont.

Lou - i - si - an - a, Lou - i - si - an - a, Lou - i - si - an - a, Ver - mont.

Lou - i - si - an - a, Lou - i - si - an - a, Ver - mont.

Lou - i - si - an - a,   Ver - mont.

Al - a - bam-a, Ar - i - zo-na, Cal - i - for-nia, Col -o - ra-do, In - di - an - a, Mas-sa -

chu-setts, Min-ne - so-ta, Mis-sis - sip-pi, Ok-la - ho-ma, Penn-syl - va-nia, Ver - mont!

Play these ostinatos as the Fifty Nifty speech piece is performed.
You may use the instruments indicated, or choose your own
instrument combinations. Play the ostinatos either throughout
the song, or during specific parts of the song.

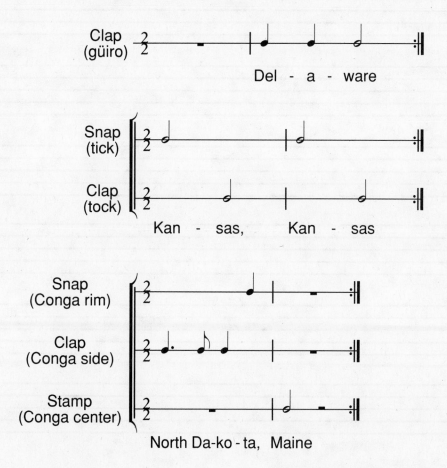

McGraw-Hill

Name

Washington Post March

by John Philip Sousa

Introduction	
	8 measures

First strain 4 times	
Second strain 4 times	
Trio	

Break strain	

Trio	all play last time

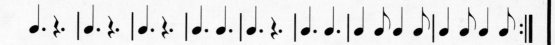

USING RESOURCE MASTER C·2

DIRECTIONS:

Distribute a copy of the Resource Master to each student. Have students find all the sections on this map that make up the march form. (introduction, first strain, second strain, trio, break strain, trio) Distribute drums, triangles, tambourines, rhythm sticks. Point out all the repeat signs before listening the first time, or playing along. You may wish to have students color the map to highlight the form. (Both trios will be the same color; other sections will be contrasting colors.)

Name _____

Made to March

John Philip Sousa (1854–1932) was born in Washington, D.C. He began his career in music at 17, by playing violin in theater and dance orchestras.

In 1880, Sousa was appointed leader of the United States Marine Band. For it he wrote many of the more than one hundred marches that made him famous. However, one of his most well-known pieces, the "Washington Post March," was composed for an entirely different purpose. During the 1880s in Washington, D.C., several newspapers were in hot competition for readers. In 1889, one of these papers, the *Washington Post*, held an essay contest for local students. John Philip Sousa was asked to write a march, named after the newspaper, to be played during the awards ceremony. The "Washington Post March" was received with enthusiasm from the moment of its debut. Marches were very much a part of the popular music of the day. The "Washington Post March" even became the favored music for a new dance style, the two-step. Although the march is one of Sousa's best-loved and most performed works, he received only $35 for the piano, band, and orchestral arrangements.

After his discharge from the Marine Corps in 1892, Sousa formed his own band. This popular group gave concerts throughout the United States and Europe and took a world tour in 1910–1911. The composer of "The Stars and Stripes Forever" and "Semper Fidelis," Sousa was a man of many talents. He also wrote songs, waltzes, orchestral suites, and tone poems, as well as five novels and his autobiography, *Marching Along*.

1. In what branch of the service did John Philip Sousa begin his military career?
2. What caused John Philip Sousa to write the "Washington Post March"?
3. Besides marches, what else did Sousa write?

(See answers at the back of this book.)

RESOURCE MASTER C•4 Script

State Your Name: Plan a Performance

In preparation for the performance of "Fifty Nifty United States," cut fifty poster board rectangles of approximately 1½ to 2 feet across. Research one or more states, label the poster board with the state's name, and decorate it with symbols important to that state. For example, Pennsylvania may have a picture of the Liberty Bell; Virginia may show its state bird, the cardinal; Arizona may have its state flower, the saguaro cactus flower. Mount each state on a handle, such as a paint stirrer.

Enter the stage in small groups, each group saying or playing one ostinato from Resource Master C•1. The last group to enter says the speech piece as the ostinato patterns continue. Everyone ends together.

Sing "America, the Beautiful" with your class to open the skit.

Walk about in the shared space holding the poster board cutouts. If you hold two cutouts, the states should be adjoining states. Substitute your home state and neighboring states for the states named in the skit below.

Student holding **MAINE** *(looks around):* Hey, New Hampshire, where are you?

NEW HAMPSHIRE *(over in a corner near Vermont):* I'm here, talking to Vermont as usual.

VERMONT: We have so much in common, you know.

MAINE *(walking up to them, gazing at others):* Who *are* all these other states, anyway?

VERMONT: The other 47. You know, the rest of the United States.

MAINE: Oh yeah? Where's California? I always wanted to see California.

CALIFORNIA *(wearing sunglasses, standing in the center near NEBRASKA and OHIO):* I'm over here.

MAINE *(MAINE, NEW HAMPSHIRE, and VERMONT move near CALIFORNIA)* Hey, how are ya?

CALIFORNIA: To tell you the truth, I'm feeling kinda crowded. I don't belong in the middle of all these states. I wonder how Nebraska and Ohio like being surrounded on all sides.

NEBRASKA: Oh, we like it in the heartland. All those amber waves of grain, that big sky country, the land of lakes, the Windy City, the Gateway to the West.

NEW HAMPSHIRE: I never really thought about how many states there are. It's quite exciting, don't you think?

VERMONT: I'd say it's nifty.

MAINE: "Nifty?" We're looking at the whole, big, beautiful United States and all you say is *"nifty"*?

VERMONT: No, I can say lots more than that. *(Steps forward and looks back at the mixed-up mass of states)* **Ready, gang? Hit it!**

Sing "Fifty Nifty United States" as you move into position. When you reach the section in the song where all 50 states are named, hold up your cutouts until you have formed a map of the United States. If you are holding a southern state, kneel and hold the cutout in front of your body. If you are holding a state in the middle or northern sections, stand and hold your cutouts higher. Raise each cutout into place as the name of that state is sung.

Try a Tê´t Trung Lantern

Vietnamese people honor the moon on the holiday of Tê´t Trung.
One of the ways children celebrate is by making colorful lanterns
to carry while marching in a parade.

Follow the directions below to create your own lantern.

Materials:

- 8½″ x 11″ piece of paper (You may want to use manila
  paper or construction paper)
- Scissors
- Staples
- Plastic tape
- Flashlight
- Crayons, markers, or paint (optional)

1. Using crayons, markers, or paint,
   decorate the paper with pictures
   of dragons, butterflies, fish,
   or hares.

2. Choose either the fish or butterfly disk
   below. Cut out the disk and the
   silhouette inside. (If you have cut through
   the edge of the disk to get to the
   silhouette, tape the edges of the circle
   together again now.)

3. Roll the paper into a cylinder the size of
   the silhouette disk. Tape or staple the
   sides of your paper where they overlap.

4. Tape the silhouette disk to the top of
   the cylinder.

5. Slip your flashlight inside the cylinder
   and turn it on. Point it at the wall in a
   darkened room and display your animal.

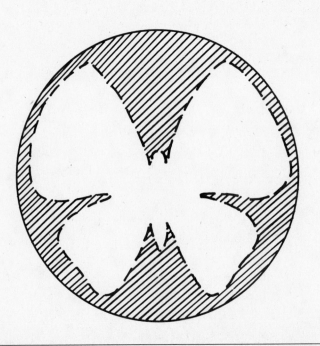

McGraw-Hill

Solar-Lunar Lore

The Story of Yi and Chang E

A long time ago, the Heavenly Emperor Jun of China was the father of ten suns. They lived in a red-flowered tree in the middle of the sea. Each morning at dawn, one of the suns would go up to the sky in a cart drawn by six dragons. When he returned at day's end, another sun would take his place the next morning. That was why people only saw one sun at a time.

After millions of years, the ten suns were tired of working alone. One morning, they all jumped into the sky at the same time. Together, they produced a strong heat that badly burned the land. The people could hardly live.

When Emperor Jun heard of this, he became angry. He sent a god named Yi to earth to discipline the suns. A good archer, Yi was given a bow and ten arrows by the Emperor. Yi and his wife, Chang E, descended to the earth and found many crops destroyed. At first Yi felt sad. He tried to scare the suns down by acting as if he were going to shoot them with the arrows. They ignored him.

Yi grew angry, and shot one sun to the ground. It turned into a golden crow. This scared the other suns, who tried to run away. Yi was too angry to let them go. He shot down several more, and as the suns disappeared, the weather cooled. People began to worry that if all the suns were gone, they would freeze. They took one of Yi's arrows so he could shoot all but the last sun. From then on, the final sun behaved well. It came out at the same time each day to warm the people and help grow crops.

The Emperor Jun did not like what Yi had done. He told Yi and Chang E they could not return to heaven. Chang E was broken-hearted. Now she would no longer be a goddess. She would grow old and die like an ordinary person. She told Yi that this was his fault. He had gotten her into trouble, and he must do something about it.

Yi thought of the Queen Mother of the West. She had a magic drink that could change things back to the way they had been. He went to visit the Queen Mother, and she gave him the magic drink. She told him that it was made from a rare fruit that grows once every 6,000 years.

Yi took the drink home to Chang E. He told her, "The Queen Mother says if two people drink this, they will live forever. If only one person drinks it, he or she will go up into the sky."

Yi thought that they should wait for a good day to drink it together. Chang E, however, thought only of herself. One night when Yi was away, Chang E drank it alone. Immediately she flew out of the window and into the sky. Thinking she would be blamed for fooling Yi, she flew to the moon palace instead of going to heaven. The palace had nothing but a bay tree and a rabbit. Chang E was very sorry about fooling her husband, but it was too late.

Since that day, people have gathered at the Mid-Autumn Festival to send Chang E a special greeting. Because she understands sadness and loneliness, they make wishes to her. She does her best to grant them.

—*Chinese Folktale*

1. Imagine this story as a drama and list the characters. Describe each person and his/her costume.
2. In this story Yi was given a problem to solve. Think about Yi's problem and develop several solutions. Share the one you like best with a classmate.
3. Chang E's decision to drink the magic drink changed her life forever. Discuss a time when you were sorry about a decision you had made.

McGraw-Hill

Name_____

Wishing for Winter

Think of words that you associate with winter and write them in the spaces provided. The categories below should help you organize your list.

Winter Weather/Scenery	Winter Sports/Fun	Winter Clothing/Other
_____	_____	_____
_____	_____	_____
_____	_____	_____
_____	_____	_____

Now write a four-line poem about winter, using some of the words you listed. Your poem does not have to rhyme. Complete the following four lines or use the remaining blank spaces to begin your poem in a different way.

Winter days are _____ ,

Winter nights are _____ ,

Winter fun is _____ ,

Winter is _____ .

_____

_____

_____

Page 2

For many people, winter means snow. Say these four rhythmic
ostinatos about snow.

Snow - flakes   are   fall - ing   ev' - ry - where.

Snow - man,   snow - man,   let's   make   a   snow - man.

Snow - balls   are   lots   of   fun,   come   on,   let's   throw   some.

Rid - ing   in   my   snow-mo - bile,   oh, what fun   to   take the wheel.

Combine all the ostinatos to create a larger piece. Transfer the
ostinatos to pitched or unpitched percussion instruments.
Use the patterns as an introduction to your poem.

Name _____

Carol Collection

O Come, All Ye Faithful

G   D7   G D7 G C G D7
1. O come, all ye faithful, joyful and triumphant,

Em   D A D G D G D A7 D
O come ye, O come ye to Bethlehem;

G   Am G D7 G   D7   A7   D7
Come and behold Him, Born the King of angels;

G   D7 G D7 G   G   D7 G C G D7
O come, let us adore Him, O come, let us adore Him,

G C   G D7 A7 D7 G C G D7   G
O come, let us adore Him, Christ, the Lord!

2. Sing, choirs of angels, sing in exultation,
Sing, all ye citizens of heaven above!
Glory to God, all glory in the highest.

O come, let us adore Him, O come, let us adore Him,
O come, let us adore Him, Christ, the Lord!

We Wish You a Merry Christmas

G   C   A7   D7
1. We wish you a Merry Christmas, We wish you a Merry Christmas,

G   C   C D7 G
We wish you a Merry Christmas, And a Happy New Year.

2. Now bring us some figgy pudding, (three times) And bring it out here.

3. For we love our figgy pudding, (three times) So bring some out here.

4. We won't go until we get some, (three times) So bring some out here.

McGraw-Hill

The First Noel

A7 D   A7   D   G D
1. The first Noel, the angel did say,

G   D   G   D   G   A7   D   A7   D
Was to certain poor shepherds in   fields as they lay;

A7 D   A7   D   G   D
In   fields where they lay keeping their sheep,

G   D   G   D G A7   D   A7 D
On a cold winter's night that was so deep.

A7 D   A7 D   G D   A7   D   G D G A7 D A7 A
Noel, Noel, Noel, Noel,   Born is the King of Is-ra-el.

2. They looked up and saw a star, Shining in the East, beyond them far,
   And to the earth it gave a great light, And so it continued both day and night.

   Noel, Noel, Noel, Noel, Born is the King of Israel.

Hark! The Herald Angels Sing

G   D7 G   C   G D7 G
Hark! the herald angels sing, "Glory to the newborn King!

G   Em A7   D   A7 D
Peace on earth, and mercy mild, God and sinners reconciled."

G   D7 G D7 G   D7 G   D7
Joyful all ye nations, rise, Join the triumph of   the skies;

C   Am E7 Am   D7   G   D7 G
With th'angelic host proclaim, "Christ is born in Bethlehem."

C   Am E7 Am   D7   G   D7 G
Hark! the herald angels sing, "Glory to the newborn King!"

Joy to the World

    D A7 G D   G D A7 D
1. Joy to the world! the Lord is come;

      G   A7   D
   Let earth receive her King;

     D G D   G   D
   Let ev'ry heart prepare Him room,

     D   A7
   And heav'n and nature sing! And heav'n and nature sing!

     D   G D   G D A7 D
   And heav'n and heav'n and nature sing.

2. Joy to the earth! the Savior reigns;
   Let men their songs employ;
   While fields and floods, rocks, hills, and plains
   Repeat the sounding joy, Repeat the sounding joy,
   Repeat, repeat the sounding joy.

O Christmas Tree

    F   C F   Gm   C7   F
O Christmas tree, O Christmas tree, With faithful leaves unchanging;

    F   C F   Gm   C7   F
O Christmas tree, O Christmas tree, With faithful leaves unchanging;

    F B♭   F Gm   Gm7 C7   F
Not only green in summer's heat, But also winter's snow and sleet,

C7 F   C F   D D7 Gm   C7   F
O Christmas tree, O Christmas tree, With faithful leaves unchanging.

Enjoy Johnnycake

Johnnycake is a type of breakfast bread popular in the Caribbean. Made with a few common ingredients, Johnnycake is fried in vegetable oil until it resembles a biscuit. It is served with fish, or bacon and eggs, or fruit such as bananas, mangos, pineapples, or oranges.

Warning: Hot oil is dangerous. Ask an adult to help you with the frying.

2 cups flour
a pinch of salt
1 tablespoon baking powder
½ teaspoon cinnamon
¼ teaspoon nutmeg
1 tablespoon butter or margarine
2 tablespoons milk
vegetable oil for frying

Mix all the dry ingredients thoroughly. Cut the butter into the dry mixture evenly, either with a pastry blender, or by pulling two knives in opposite directions, back and forth through the dough. Sprinkle the milk over the dough before kneading it. If it is too sticky, gradually add more flour; if it is too dry, add some cold water, by teaspoonfuls, until you feel it is easier to work with the dough.

Roll a chunk of dough until it resembles the size and shape of a golf ball, then flatten slightly. Continue in this way until all the Johnnycakes have been formed.

Now you are ready to fry the Johnnycakes. Ask an older friend or adult to help you.

Deep-fry until both sides are golden brown. Allow the Johnnycakes to cool for a few minutes; serve them warm or at room temperature.

Kwanzaa: Community Time for Values

Kwanzaa is a holiday for African Americans to celebrate who they are and from where they come. Much of the celebrating takes place within family gatherings, although many cities and towns have community events throughout the seven days of the holiday. There is no single way to celebrate Kwanzaa. What is important is gathering together, sharing important ideas and a reverence for life, honoring the past, and celebrating all that is good.

When Dr. Maulana Karenga created Kwanzaa, he included seven principles, called the Nguzo Saba, to help remember important values. The Nguzo Saba combine African traditions with African American ideals. Each night of Kwanzaa provides an opportunity to explore, think about, and discuss these principles.

Read the seven principles of Kwanzaa listed below. Discuss them with your classmates, and give examples of how a person might follow each principle.

1. **UMOJA** (UNITY): To try to achieve unity and harmony in the family and community.

2. **KUJICHAGULIA** (SELF-DETERMINATION): To speak for ourselves instead of letting others tell us who we are and how we should be.

3. **UJIMA** (COLLECTIVE WORK AND RESPONSIBILITY): To build and maintain our community and solve our sisters' and brothers' problems together.

4. **UJAMAA** (COOPERATIVE ECONOMICS): To build our businesses together in order to maintain the economy of our community.

5. **NIA** (PURPOSE): To build and develop our community to restore our people to their traditional greatness.

6. **KUUMBA** (CREATIVITY): To always leave our community better than when we inherited it.

7. **IMANI** (FAITH): To believe in our people, our leaders, our teachers, and our parents, and the righteousness and victory of our struggle.

Dream His Dream: Plan a Performance

Plan a performance that includes an excerpt from Martin Luther King's "I Have a Dream" speech. Choose songs such as "I Wish I Knew How It Would Feel to Be Free," "The Dream of Martin Luther King," "Free at Last," and "Lift Every Voice and Sing" to begin and end your program.

Choose seven speakers to deliver portions of the speech and narrative below. Select songs to begin and end the program.

Speaker 1: One hundred years after President Abraham Lincoln signed the Emancipation Proclamation and freed the slaves, African Americans were still denied many of their civil rights.

Speaker 2: On August 28, 1963, 200,000 people gathered at the Lincoln Memorial in Washington, D.C. They came to show their support for Civil Rights, insisting that all Americans be guaranteed what the Constitution promised—life, liberty, and the pursuit of happiness.

Speaker 3: The Civil Rights Movement was a high point in our nation's history, with Americans of all cultural backgrounds united to begin correcting injustices of the past.

Speaker 4: That day in 1963, Dr. Martin Luther King, Jr. delivered a speech that will long be remembered in the minds and hearts of Americans—"I Have a Dream." (pause) He said: *(Play the recording of the excerpt from "I Have a Dream.")*

Speaker 5: Dr. King knew that working for freedom was a hard task. In the face of hatred and opposition, he persevered, believing that his life might make a difference.

Speaker 6: Five years after this speech, Dr. King was struck down by an assassin's bullet at the age of 39. At his funeral, Dr. Benjamin Mays said: "If we love Martin Luther King and respect him, as this crowd surely testifies, let us see to it that he did not die in vain. Martin Luther King, Jr.'s unfinished work on earth must truly be our own."

Speaker 7: In this spirit, we invite you to join us in song.

Sound and Silence

Fill in each beat. Use quarter notes, quarter rests, and pairs of eighth notes. Play your rhythms.

Echo-clap each pattern you hear, then write it below. (Your teacher will play patterns with quarter notes, quarter rests, and pairs of eighth notes.) Play the patterns on percussion instruments with "Music Brings Us Together!"

McGraw-Hill

Pitches in Two Keys

Imitate four-beat ascending and descending patterns of *do re mi* by singing and using hand signs.

Read the melody shown below.

1. Say the rhythm.

2. Clap the rhythm.

3. Sing the pitches using pitch syllables and hand signs.

4. Write the pitch syllables under each note.

Write the above exercise in the key of F major. Observe that when *do* and *mi* are on spaces, then *re* is on the line between them.

Name_____

Writing *do re mi*

Write the pitch syllables and letter names for these pitches.

Fill in the notes missing from "Good News." Listen to the song.

Write the pitch syllables and letter names for these pitches. Then write the three pitches in a different order and label them.

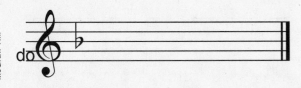

Practice with Rhythms

Practice the conducting pattern for $\frac{4}{4}$.

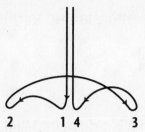

2   1 4   3

Write three different four-beat combinations in the measures below.
Use combinations of these rhythms:

  ♩ = 2 beats   ▬ = 2 beats   ♩ = 1 beat

         𝄾 = 1 beat   ♫ = 1 beat

The last measure already contains a four-beat **whole note** for a definite "ending"
feeling. The feeling of ending is called a cadence.

$\frac{4}{4}$ __ __ __ __ | __ __ __ __ | __ __ __ 𝅝 __ __ __ |

Practice playing your rhythm as a partner conducts you. Now write four different
four-beat combinations in the measures below. Use combinations of these rhythms:

            𝅝 = 4 beats   ▬ = 4 beats

            ♩ = 2 beats   ▬ = 2 beats

            ♩ = 1 beat   𝄾 = 1 beat

                    ♫ = 1 beat

Use the whole rest (▬) in either measure 2 or 3.

$\frac{4}{4}$ __ __ __ __ | __ __ __ __ | __ __ __ __ | __ __ __ __ |

Recognize and Write Syncopation

Does the syncopated pattern ♪♩♪ appear in the following songs?

Circle Yes or No for each song listed below.

"America, the Beautiful," page 172	Yes	No
"Shabat Shalom," page 125	Yes	No
"We Will Raise a Ruckus Tonight," page 20	Yes	No
"Adongko Dongko A Gakit," page 43	Yes	No
"Yankee Doodle," page 139	Yes	No
"Something to Sing About," page 174	Yes	No

Fill in each measure below with four beats of rhythm notation. Use the syncopated pattern ♪♩♪ or ♪♪♩♪♪ in each measure. The syncopated pattern takes up two beats, but it can occur on different beats in the measure. If you use the syncopation in beats 2 and 3, use ♪♪♩♪♪ instead of ♪♩♪

Play your pattern on a drum with "Funga Alafia."

$\frac{4}{4}$ _ _ _ _ | _ _ _ _ | _ _ _ _ | _ _ _ _ |

Practice with the Pentatonic Scale

"Li'l 'Liza Jane" is a pentatonic melody.
Notice how it uses both a low and a high *do*.

do re mi so la do'

Draw lines to match the words of "Li'l 'Liza Jane"
to the melodic patterns.

She's the one that I adore

mi mi re do

Li'l 'Liza Jane

do' so la so

There's a gal in Baltimore

la so mi so

O Eliza

mi mi re do mi so so

Li'l 'Liza Jane

mi mi re do mi so so

McGraw-Hill

Musical Concentration

Form partners. Each partner cuts out a complete set of cards. Combine all cards and place facedown. Take turns turning over two cards at a time. When a matching pair is found, the other person is to sing those notes. If sung accurately, that person takes the pair. Use a pitched instrument to check for pitch accuracy. If not sung accurately, the first person gets the cards. If the cards do not match, turn them facedown again. The winner is the person with the most pairs when all matches have been made.

At the end of the game, arrange several cards to compose original melodies. Play the melodies on a pitched instrument.

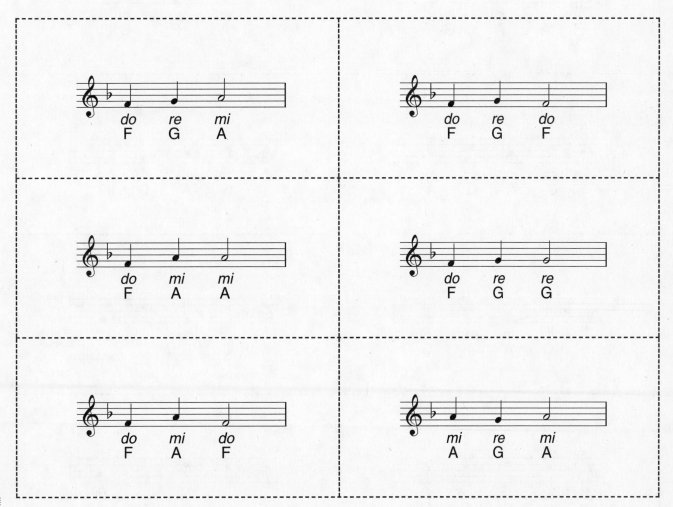

Musical Concentration (page 2)

mi   re   do
A   G   F

mi   do   mi
A   F   A

mi   mi   re
A   A   G

mi   do   re
A   F   G

so   mi   so   mi
C   A   C   A

so   mi   re   do
C   A   G   F

so   mi   do   re
C   A   F   G

so   do   so   do
C   F   C   F

so   la   so   la
C   D   C   D

so   la   so   mi
C   D   C   A

Musical Concentration (page 3)

so la mi do
C D A F

so la so do
C D C F

do so la so
F C D C

mi do mi do
A F A F

la so la so
D C D C

la so mi so
D C A C

mi re mi re
A G A G

mi so mi so
A C A C

mi la so mi
A D C A

so mi
C A

RESOURCE MASTER R•8 Practice

Recognize a Dotted Rhythm

Find the dotted quarter notes (♩.) in this countermelody to "Hong Tsai Me Me." The dotted quarter note lasts the same as a quarter note tied to an eighth note.

Read the rhythm.

Compare the rhythm of measures 1, 3, 5, and 7 with the tinted pattern in "Sweet Potatoes," page 86.

Sing the countermelody alone and then with "Hong Tsai Me Me."

"Hong Tsai Me Me" Countermelody

Countermelody by Marilyn C. Davidson

Rain - bow sis - ter, kind and good.

I would see her if I could.

Can't for - get her, Don't know why,

Think - ing of her, I al - ways cry.

McGraw-Hill

"Gau Shan Ching" Countermelody

Play or sing this countermelody with "Gau Shan Ching," page 74.

1. Read the rhythm.
2. Sing the pitch syllables using hand signs.
3. Sing with letter names.
4. Sing or play the part on recorder, bells, or other pitched instruments.

To sing or play with the recording, wait for the four-measure introduction, play the countermelody three times, then listen to the coda without playing or singing.

"Gau Shan Ching" Countermelody

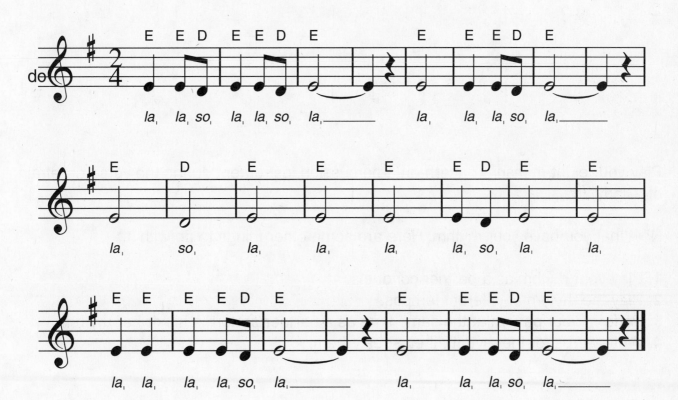

McGraw-Hill

Create with Sixteenth-Note Combinations

Complete the measures below so that there are two beats in every measure. Empty beats are indicated with a dash (____). Use each of these rhythms at least once.

♫ = four sixteenths = 1 beat divided into four equal parts

♫ = dotted eighth and sixteenth = 1 beat divided into four equal parts with the first three parts tied together

♫ = two sixteenths and an eighth = 1 beat divided into four equal parts with the last two parts tied together

Play your eight-measure pattern on a percussion instrument during the verse or refrain of "Cindy."

Now that you have your rhythm. Here are some other things to do with it.

1. Play your rhythm as a partner conducts.
2. Play the rhythm at different tempos.
3. Perform your pattern at the same time as a partner performs his or her rhythm.
4. Write words for the rhythm, then speak them.

Melodies with *fa*

Fill in the missing pitch syllables. Then name the tunes. Remember that if *mi* and *so* are on lines, *fa* is in the space between those two lines.

Title: _____

do ___ do do ___ do mi ___ so ___ mi ___ so

Write this melody in C major. Play it on a pitched instrument.

do re mi fa so so so   so fa mi re do do do

Play the melody using F as *do*. Then write it below in the key of F. What signature will you need to add?

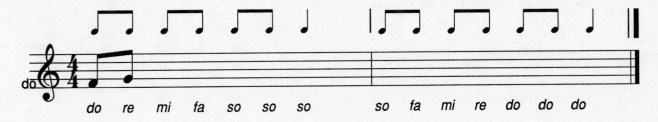

do re mi fa so so so   so fa mi re do do do

McGraw-Hill

Two Key Signatures

For each song listed below, fill in the number of flats and sharps in the key signature and the letter name of *do*.

Song	Key Signature (number of flats or sharps)	*Do*
"Mango Walk" page 70	_____	_____
"Sweet Potatoes" page 86	_____	_____
"Song of Peace" page 137	_____	_____
"Something to Sing About" page 174	_____	_____
"New York, New York" page 212	_____	_____
"Tzena, Tzena" page 396	_____	_____

What is the key signature of songs when *do* = C? _____

What is the key signature of songs when *do* = F? _____

Name _____

Tonal Center

The tonal center is a pitched resting place in music. It is the home tone of a scale. The tonal center can be approached from above or below.

Find the tonal center of each song fragment shown.
1. Sing each example.
2. Decide whether the missing note is higher or lower than the last note shown.
3. Fill in the missing note—the tonal center and identify it as *do* or *la*.

Hot Cross Buns

Hot cross buns.   Hot cross buns.   One a pen-ny, two a pen-ny, hot cross____

Yankee Doodle

Stuck a feath-er   in   his cap and called it mac-a- ____ ____

The Star-Spangled Banner

O'er the   land____ of the free   and the   home   of the   ____

Funga Alafia

mi mi   re ____

Zum gali gali

do re mi   mi   re   do ti₁ ____

McGraw-Hill

RESOURCE MASTER R•14 Practice

Value of Sixteenth Notes

Use this chart as a reference for various rhythms.

Compare the notes in both columns. The beamed notes on the left are equal to the tied notes on the right.

Write eight measures of rhythm using sixteenth-note rhythms as well as other rhythms.

Use [beamed notes], [beamed notes], and [beamed notes] at least once in your composition.

Play the measures on unpitched percussion instruments.

Use with page 386. • Grade 5

McGraw-Hill

Upbeats and Incomplete Measures

A song or phrase may start on a weak beat, called an upbeat. When a song begins with an upbeat, there will be an incomplete measure at the end. The first measure of the piece begins on the first downbeat.

Circle the upbeats and the incomplete measure in each example.

Check your answers. Write the circled beats from each example above in one of the boxes. All measures below should contain four beats.

1.

2.

3.

4.

Make up your own pattern. Include an upbeat at the beginning and an incomplete measure at the end (where you see the question marks). Use these rhythms:

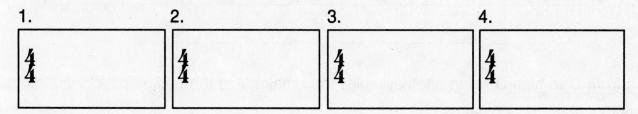

C-Major Patterns

In C major, the half steps are between E and F (*mi* and *fa*) and
between B and C (*ti* and high *do*).

1. Sing the examples below using pitch syllables and hand signs.
2. Write in the letter names below the notation.
3. Sing the melodies using letter names.

Sing from D to high D using pitch syllables in D major. Are the half steps in the same

places as they are in C major? _____

Why or why not? _____

Play the letter names from D to high D on bells. Are the half steps in the same places

as in C major? _____

Why or why not? _____

Name_____

RESOURCE MASTER R•17 Practice

Bell and Recorder Parts for "The Thing"

Write the pitch syllable for each pitch in the
C-major scale. Circle the pitches that are
a half step apart.

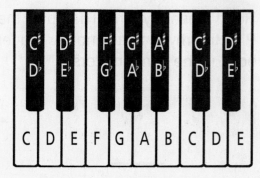

Notice the lines in the bell part that are repeated.
Sing the part with pitch syllables. What do you notice about the first line?
Play the part on bells with "The Thing."

Bell Part to "The Thing"

Play the part on recorder with "The Thing."

Recorder Part to "The Thing"

McGraw-Hill

Name_____

Reading in Two Meters

Read these rhythms. Then play them on percussion instruments.
Play the rhythms as another student conducts. Find songs in your
book in the same meters.

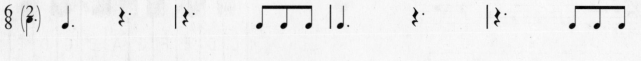

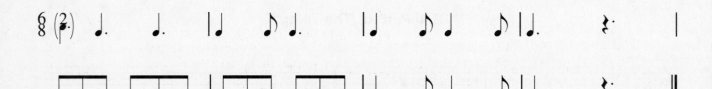

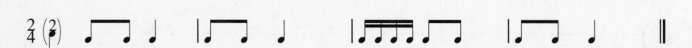

Singing in ⅜ with *ti*

Sing these words to the tune of "Row, Row, Row Your Boat."

> *"Do do do re mi*, not my cut of tea.
> Start it on *so* and we'll let it all go with the solfège family."

Add this harmony part.

Sing the harmony part with words, then pitch syllables. Notice the pitch syllable *ti*.
Play the part on bells as written, in C. Then try playing it in G. What do you need to do?

Write the harmony part using G as *do*. Place the sharp sign on the fifth line at the beginning of each staff to show that the key is G major.

Play it on bells.

RESOURCE MASTER R•20 Practice

Work in E Minor

Fill in the missing letter names and pitch syllables for each example below.
Sing the melodies with pitch syllables.

Can you name these songs?

Building Chords and Writing Melodies Based on Chords

Complete the chords. Name the pitches
needed and write in both the pitch syllables
and letter names.

Draw the notes for the chords on the staff.
Notes for chords are written directly above
one another.

Harmony (Chords)   Melody

Complete the notation below to create a new musical phrase.
For the melody, use any pitches of the I chord (C E G) or of the V chord (G B D).
Use the set of pitches that goes with the chords names in the harmony part.
Fill in the chord pitches to complete the harmony part.
Work with a partner. Play your music on bells.

Creating, Writing, and Playing with Sixteenth Notes

Create an eight-measure rhythm using these:

Play your rhythm with rhythm sticks.
Stems up show tapping sticks alternately on the floor.

Stems down show clicking sticks together in the air.

Write your rhythm above the beat bars.
Play your rhythm as an accompaniment with the refrains of "Going to Boston" and "Cindy." Revise your accompaniment as needed.

$\frac{2}{4}$

McGraw-Hill

Dotted Eighth Notes

Compare these two patterns: ♪♬ and ♬ The dotted eighth-sixteenth note pattern divides the beat unequally and the two eighths pattern divides the beat equally.

♪♬ = ♪♪♪♪

♬ = ♪♪ ♪♪

Change pairs of eighth notes to dotted eighth-sixteenth patterns in "Wondering." (Add the dot and the short beam.) Then sing the song using this rhythm.

Wondering

Bohemian Folk Song

1. Where are the clouds that were here last night?
2. How far a - way is the dis - tant sky?

Why does the moon give a sil - v'ry light?
How do we know which is you or I?

Who can tell? Who can say?
Who can tell? Who can say?

When will to - mor - row be yes - ter day?
How man - y miles would be far a - way?

A Blues Bass Line

Play this blues bass line with "The City Blues."

Practice the bass line on this keyboard. Then take turns playing it on any pitched instrument. Use a low-sounding instrument if possible.

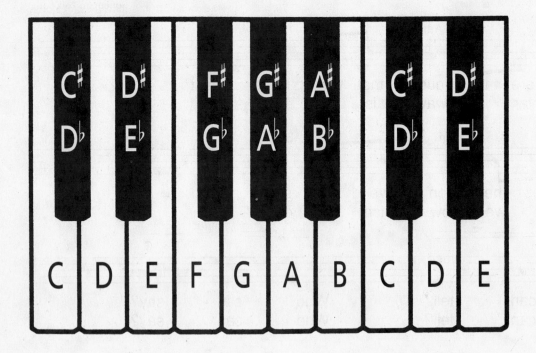

Use I-IV-V Chords

Write the letters of the chord roots. This song is in G major.

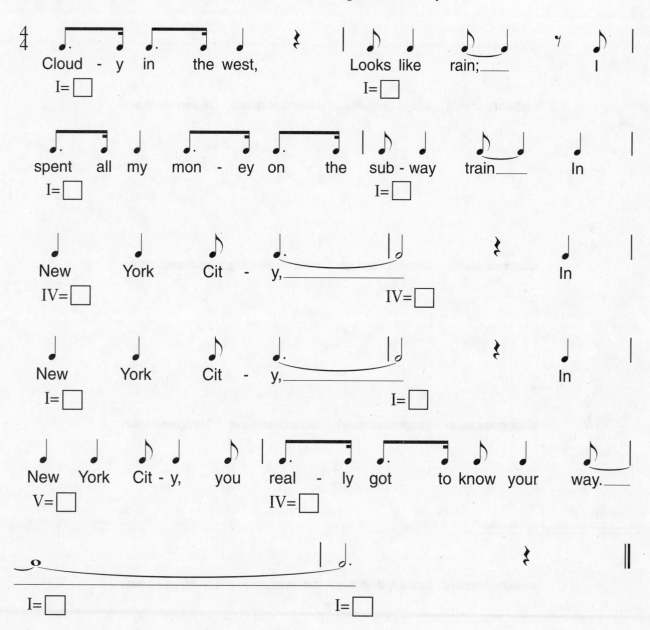

Sing the chord roots with the song. Play the chords on autoharps or
other chording instruments.

RESOURCE MASTER R•26 Transparency Master

Beat Bars

▬▬ ▬▬ ▬▬ ▬▬

▬▬ ▬▬ ▬▬ ▬▬

▬▬ ▬▬ ▬▬ ▬▬

▬▬ ▬▬ ▬▬ ▬▬

Name_____

Pitch Ladder

Curwen Hand Signs

do

ti

la

so

fa

mi

re

do

Name

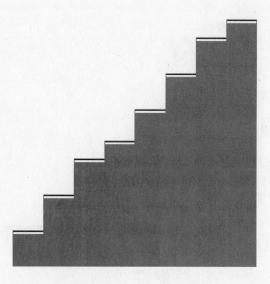

TEACHER: Write in pitches as needed. This stairstep goes from low *do* to high *do*.

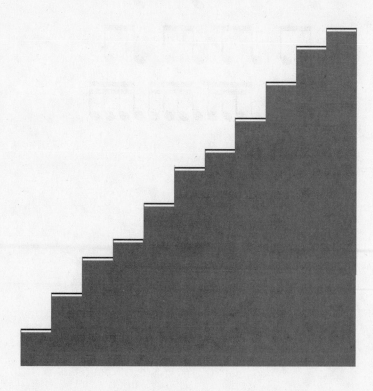

TEACHER: Write in pitches as needed. This stairstep goes from low *so* to high *do*.

McGraw-Hill

Note Values

TEACHER: Have students add other note values to the chart.

Scale Brackets

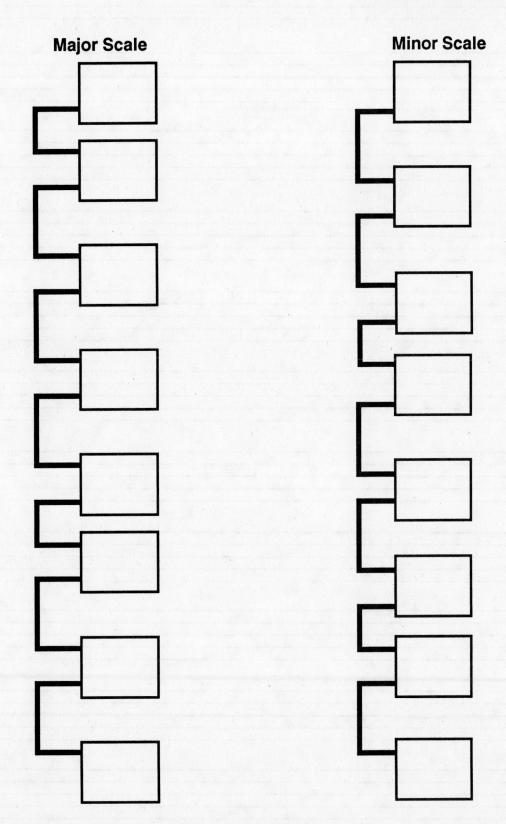

Major Scale

Minor Scale

TEACHER: Give students a starting pitch and have them create a major or minor scale by writing pitch letter names in the boxes.

McGraw-Hill

Gaudeamus omnes
Gregorian Chant

McGraw-Hill

USING RESOURCE MASTER LA·1

DIRECTIONS:

Distribute a copy of the Resource Master to each student. Have students find the three main sections of the listening map, labeled A, B, and A. Tell them that each curved line represents one sung phrase, and each apostrophe represents a break between phrases. Direct students' attention to the B section and explain that the map shows the alternation between the small group singing and the choir singing. Ask students which lines are sung by the small group and which are sung by the choir in this section. (Lines 1 and 3 are sung by the small group; Lines 2, 4, and 5 are sung by the choir) Explain that the Latin word at the top of each section is the first word heard in that section. Point out the dynamic markings before listening. You may wish to have students color the A sections one color and the B section another color to highlight the form.

Brandenburg Concerto No. 2, Third Movement
by Johann Sebastian Bach

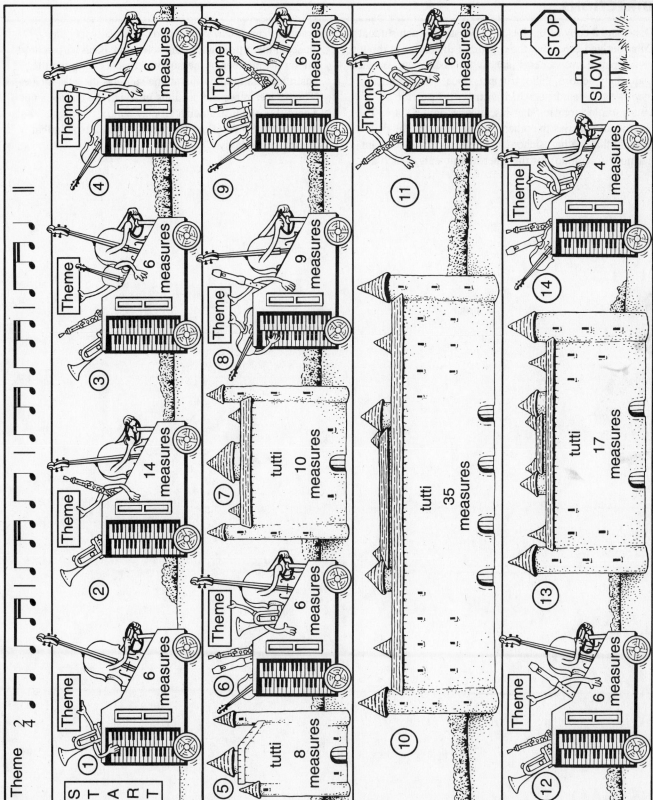

McGraw-Hill Listening Map concept by Debra Erck

USING RESOURCE MASTER LA·2

DIRECTIONS:

Distribute a copy of the Resource Master to each student. Point out and echo-clap the rhythm of the theme at the top of the map. Have students identify the instruments on the map. (harpsichord, cello, trumpet, oboe, violin, and recorder) Ask students which instruments provide transportation for the other instruments on the map. (The harpsichord carries the others and is driven by the cello.) Explain that the harpsichord and cello form the constant harmony (continuo) for the other instruments, which are

soloists. They "carry" the solos, musically, playing beneath them throughout the selection. Each harpsichord shows the number of measures in that section, and the instrument(s) holding the theme sign has the solo theme. The palaces represent sections in which the theme is not heard, but the instruments all play contrasting material at various times. Point out the word *tutti* and explain that it means "everybody."

Name _____

Trumpet Concerto in E♭, First Movement
by Franz Joseph Haydn

USING RESOURCE MASTER LA·3

DIRECTIONS:

Distribute a copy of the Resource Master to each student. Have the students locate the main sections on the map. (A A' B A" cadenza, closing) Ask the students which section does not contain the theme. (B) Next have them tell if the orchestra or the trumpet is featured in the various sections. (A: orchestra; A' : trumpet; B: both trumpet and orchestra; A": trumpet; cadenza: trumpet; closing: orchestra) Explain that the cadenza is a special section near the end of a concerto movement, featuring the solo instrument without orchestral accompaniment. Play the theme on a pitched instrument before playing the recording so that the students will recognize it when they hear it within the orchestra. You may wish to have students color all the A sections one color, and the other sections contrasting colors, to highlight the form.

Name _____

Polonaise in A Major Op. 40, No. 1
(Military Polonaise)

by Frédéric François Chopin

USING RESOURCE MASTER LA·4

DIRECTIONS:

Distribute a copy of the Resource Master to each student. Have students echo-clap the theme at the top of the map. Explain that each triangle in the A section represents one measure. The dancers are shown in different poses to represent the a b a parts of the A section. In the c parts of the B section, the general contour of the melody is shown for each beat by the placement of the number of the beat on the staff when the music gets too complex to show the actual score. In the d part of the B section, just the rhythm is shown. Be sure to point out and explain the *Da Capo al Fine* (go back to the beginning), *no repeat,* and the *Fine* (end), giving a form of A B A. You may wish to have students color the A triangle one color, and the B circle another color, to highlight the form.

Sanctus from *Requiem*
by Gabriel Urbain Fauré

McGraw-Hill Listening Map concept by Debbie Tannert

USING RESOURCE MASTER LA·5

DIRECTIONS:

Distribute a copy of the Resource Master to each student. Help students find and identify all the instruments on the map. (introduction: violin, harp; before last line: French horn and harp; above last row: two French horns; coda: violin and harp) Point out the pictures of a boy and a man at the beginning of each row. Explain that the boys sing the higher parts (soprano), and the men sing the lower parts (tenor), as shown in the key at the top of the map. Point out the arrangement of the words of the text, and the way the upper line overlaps the lower line on much of the map. Explain that, at these points in the recording, the upper voices and lower voices overlap in their singing of the text. Have students find all of the dynamic markings on the listening map before playing the recording.

Name _____

String Quartet in B Minor, Fourth Movement
by Teresa Carreño

McGraw-Hill Listening Map concept by Barb Stevenson

USING RESOURCE MASTER LA·6

DIRECTIONS:

Distribute a copy of the Resource Master to each student. Have students find all the lettered sections on the map (A B A'). Echo-clap each of the three main rhythm patterns on the map. Point out the words describing the music in the various parts of each section. Have students identify each instrument pictured. (A section: cello, viola; B section: violin, cello, cello, violin; A' section: viola, two violins, cello, cello, violin) Point out and explain the *rit.* marking (getting slower) and the *a tempo* marking. (back to the original speed) The number of measures in each part is indicated on the map to help keep track of elapsed time. Have students locate all the dynamic markings on the map before listening. You may wish to have students color the A and A' triangles one color, and the B circle another color, to highlight the form.

Possibilities

A musical revue with 12 sequences
by Teresa Jennings

CAST

Grade 5 singers
Grade K–4 singers for "Big Dreams" (*optional*)
Grade 6–8 singers for "It's My Journey" (*optional*)
Speakers (*approximately 49 "lines" that can be assigned in a variety of ways*)
Professional people (*in costume*)**:** Doctor, Business Executive, Astronaut, Mountain Climber, Author, Film Director, Dancer, Musician, Scientist, Singer, Professional Athlete, Journalist, Computer Developer

---

Time: the present
Place: school auditorium

SEQUENCE 1: SONG

(Performers and singers enter.)

SONG: "Possibilities"

(Singers who are doing the movements quickly exit stage right and stage left after the applause.)

SEQUENCE 2: NARRATION

(Speakers enter stage left and stage right, forming a semicircle center stage.)

Speaker 1: Hello, friends! And welcome to our show! As you have heard, we have a lot to say about the subject of possibilities.

Speaker 2: Just think about the choices we have in our lives. There's no limit to what we can think about and learn about.

Speaker 3: We can go to school to learn, but we can also learn from our experiences and from other people.

Speaker 4: We can think about anything we want to, anytime we want to, because our minds are our own.

Speaker 5: We can read books, talk to people, watch movies, study, or just plain think so we will grow.

McGraw-Hill

Speaker 6: When we talk about possibilities, we aren't just talking about physical possibilities. We're talking about the possibilities of what is deep inside each of us.

Speaker 7: We're talking about things like growth, wisdom, peace of mind, and happiness. Those are things that come from who we are, not what we look like.

Speaker 8: They don't come from how much money we have, or where we were born. They come from inside us, and each of us is unique.

Speaker 9: As the song says, our lives are spread out before us, and we can see so many possibilities.

Speaker 10: The toughest part of having so many possibilities is deciding which ones we will pursue. It's like picking out a birthday present!

Speaker 11: From the time we are born, we are already reaching out to make choices for ourselves.

Speaker 12: Even little kids have dreams—big dreams!

(Speakers exit. Fifth grade singers and/or primary students for next sequence move to right and left wings.)

SEQUENCE 3: SONG

(Selected singers enter from right and left to perform the next song center stage. During the song, Speakers 1 and 2, Doctor, Business Executive, Astronaut, Mountain Climber get ready in left wing. Speaker 3, Author, Film Director, Dancer, Speaker 4, and Musician get ready in right wing.)

SONG: "Big Dreams"

SEQUENCE 4: NARRATION

(After the applause, the primary singers exit the performance area, or, if they are fifth graders, return to their positions. Speakers 1 and 2, Doctor, Business Executive, Astronaut, and Mountain Climber enter and stand stage left; Speaker 3, Author, Film Director, Dancer, Musician, and Speaker 4 enter and stand stage right.)

Speaker 1: Everyone has big dreams at some time or other.

Speaker 2: Most of the time, when we think of our dreams, we think about our abilities.

(Doctor, Business Executive, Astronaut, Mountain Climber, Author, Film Director, and Speaker 3 take two steps forward together.)

Doctor: *(stepping forward)* For example, we think about becoming doctors . . .

Business Executive: *(stepping forward)* . . . or starting our own business.

Astronaut: *(stepping forward)* Maybe we will think about traveling in space. . .

Mountain Climber: *(stepping forward)* . . . or climbing mountains.

Author: *(stepping forward)* Maybe we will write books . . .

Film Director: *(stepping forward)* . . . or make movies.

(Doctor, Business Executive, Astronaut, Mountain Climber, Author, Film Director, and Speaker 2 take three steps back. Dancer, Musician, Speaker 3, and Speaker 4 take two steps forward together.)

Speaker 3: Whatever our dreams are, we are probably already thinking about them now. In fact, lots of people start working on their dreams as soon as they can.

Dancer: *(stepping forward)* Dancers might begin to take lessons when they are very young.

Musician: *(stepping forward)* Musicians might start to learn about music in grade school or middle school.

Speaker 4: We have some performers right here at our school who are already working on their dreams, too!

(speakers exit)

SEQUENCE 5: OPTIONAL SHOWCASE

(Performers and speakers enter, perform, and exit.)

[The "Sequence 5: Optional Showcase" is meant to be a section of the musical that is totally up to the music teacher. It is a Student Talent Showcase. Dancers, singers, instrumentalists, comedians, orchestra, band, choir could be featured. An example of an introduction could be: The Monroe Street Elementary and Middle School Kazoo ensemble will not only demonstrate their musical abilities, but also their political aspirations by performing "Hail to the Chief." The pieces would tie in with possibilities, careers, future, and so on.]

(Speakers 5 through 12 move to left wing during the last performance of optional Sequence 5. Scientist, Singer, Professional Athlete, Author, Computer Developer move to right wing.)

SEQUENCE 6: NARRATION

(After the applause, Speakers 5 through 12 enter from stage left. Scientist, Singer, Professional Athlete, Author, Computer Developer enter, stage right.)

Speaker 5: As you have seen—and heard—we all have big dreams in common.

Speaker 6: But there's no rule that says we cannot have more than one dream.

Speaker 7: Or that we cannot change our minds!

Speaker 8: Our decisions about our own lives are part of our many possibilities.

Speaker 9: Of course, as long as we're dreaming, we might as well think of as much as we can!

Speaker 10: There is no limit to the possibilities we all have.

Speaker 11: When we think of possibilities as careers, jobs, or occupations, the sky is the limit.

Speaker 12: We might choose to narrow it down a little to the things we would find appealing.

Scientist: *(stepping forward)* If I'm good at science, I might think about becoming a scientist.

Singer: *(stepping forward)* If I can sing, I might think about becoming a performer.

Professional Athlete: *(stepping forward)* If I am good at sports, I might become a professional athlete.

Journalist: *(stepping forward)* If I like to read or write, maybe I will become a journalist.

Computer Developer: *(stepping forward)* If my computer is my favorite thing, maybe I will write programs or invent my own computer someday.

All: But for now, it sure is fun to think about anything and everything!

(They take their places with the singers.)

SEQUENCE 7: SONG

SONG: "I'm Gonna Be"

SEQUENCE 8: NARRATION

(After the applause, the speakers for this sequence come to the front of the performance area.)

Speaker 1: Did you know that everything we do in life is a choice?

Speaker 2: Of course, we can't choose the way other people act or things happen. But we can choose the way *we* will be.

Speaker 3: As we said before, we can choose our occupations. We can choose our dreams. But our possibilities are so much more than that.

Speaker 4: We have the possibility to choose whether we will smile or frown. We have the possibility to choose whether to let things bother us or not.

Speaker 5: Sometimes things on the outside of us can hurt us and we need to cry. There's nothing wrong with that. It's perfectly normal.

Speaker 6: But most of the things that happen around us every day are things we can choose how to feel about.

Speaker 7: If somebody says something to you that isn't nice, you can choose to get angry or hurt, or you can choose to ignore it.

Speaker 8: If you get a grade you don't like, you can choose to improve yourself for next time. If the sky is cloudy and gray, you can carry your own sunshine!

Speaker 9: It isn't always easy to let things roll off you, especially things that hurt. But sooner or later, even these things will pass. What won't pass is your ability to choose.

Speaker 10: It's important that we all know about our own possibilities in life. The point is, your choices are yours. Your life is yours. Your dreams are yours.

Speaker 11: Whatever happens in life, you have the power to choose *how* you will be. You have the power to keep dreaming. And you can choose to believe in yourself.

Speaker 12: You can choose to know who you are and where you are going. Trust in yourself and your faith will show through.

McGraw-Hill

Speaker 13: Remember: don't ever give up. *You* are worth it!

(Speakers return to chorus.)

SEQUENCE 9: SONG

SONG: "Don't Ever Give Up"

SEQUENCE 10: UNDERSCORE/NARRATION

INSTRUMENTAL: "Underscore Music"/Narration

(The speakers go to the front of the performance area and deliver their lines during the performance of the underscore music.)

Speaker 1: There's an old saying that life is a journey, a road to be traveled.

Speaker 2: If it's true, what an adventure it could be!

Speaker 3: It could be full of beautiful mountains to climb and peaceful valleys to cross.

Speaker 4: There could be days of warming sunshine and days of cooling rain.

Speaker 5: One day we might choose a path that brings us to a whole new place.

Speaker 6: But each and every day on that journey could be special.

Speaker 7: That's the most important thing to remember.

Speaker 8: There are possibilities all along the way.

Speaker 9: If we hurry through trying to reach our destinations, we're missing the best parts.

Speaker 10: It's up to us to figure out how to appreciate them.

Speaker 11: It's up to us to remember that each day will happen only once.

Speaker 12: After all, each one of us has a journey to take . . .

All: . . . and the *possibilities* are endless!

(Speakers join chorus for "It's My Journey.")

McGraw-Hill

SEQUENCE 11: SONG

SONG: "It's My Journey!"

(All cast members quickly return to the stage, the youngest in front, for the Bow Music.)

SEQUENCE 12: PLAYOFF

INSTRUMENTAL: "Playoff" ("It's My Journey!" reprise)

(During this bow music, each row takes hands and moves forward three steps, counting "One, two, three, bow!" so that all bow at once. Each row then separates in the middle and quickly leaves the stage as the next row comes forward.)

Student _____ Date _____

Portfolio Evaluation Form

Directions: For each student, review the contents of the portfolio and assign a score of 1–4 for each criterion listed below. Determine a summary score for the entire portfolio, based on Criteria 1–12 (or more).

	Needs to Improve	Fair	Good	Excellent
CONTENTS				
1. **Completeness.** Meets all requirements.	1	2	3	4
2. **Variety.** Includes a variety of pieces.	1	2	3	4
3. **Organization.** Shows clear organizational plan.	1	2	3	4
4. **Volume.** Includes sufficient amount of work.	1	2	3	4
5. **Focus/Purpose.** Meets intended purposes.	1	2	3	4
ATTRIBUTES				
6. **Effort.** Demonstrates concerted effort.	1	2	3	4
7. **Quality.** Illustrates appropriate level of quality.	1	2	3	4
8. **Creativity.** Shows imagination and creative ideas.	1	2	3	4
9. **Risk-Taking.** Takes risks in creating/choosing works that go beyond minimum expectations.	1	2	3	4
10. **Growth.** Shows improvement.	1	2	3	4
11. **Reflection.** Shows signs of personal reflection.	1	2	3	4
12. **Self-Evaluation.** Shows awareness of strengths and weaknesses.	1	2	3	4

THINGS YOU'D LIKE TO ADD

13. _____	1	2	3	4
14. _____	1	2	3	4
15. _____	1	2	3	4

SUMMARY SCORE

Meets the requirements of program goals.	1	2	3	4

COMMENTS

RESOURCE MASTER TA•2 Tools for Assessment

Student Assessment Cards

Directions: Have students complete one or more of these cards as an attachment for each item chosen for their portfolios.

Name of piece _____ Date _____

My description of this piece

Name of piece _____ Date _____

Why I like this piece

How I might change this piece

Name of piece _____ Date _____

What I learned from doing this

Name _____ Date _____

Interest Inventory

Put a check beside as many answers as you like.

1. I like to. . .

_____ listen to music   _____ move to music

_____ play music   _____ compose music

_____ sing songs   _____ perform for others

2. Types of music I like are. . .

_____

_____

_____

3. I'd like to know more about. . .

4. Here's an idea I'd like to try in music. . .

RESOURCE MASTER TA•4 Tools for Assessment

Self-Assessment Form

What I can do well	What I would like to do better
in listening	
in playing music	
in singing	
in moving to music	
in composing music	
in performing for others	

I'd like you to know. . .

Name _____ Grade _____

Music Log

Date	Title	What I Thought About It

Answer Key

Resource Master 1•2, Page 3

1. d. 2. a. 3. b. 4. e. 5. c.

6. G A B G 8. B A B G 10. G A G B

7. A G B G 9. A G G B

Resource Master 1•3, Page 4

1. F A G F
do mi re do

2. G B G A
do mi do re

3. B G A G
mi do re do

4. A A G F
mi mi re do

5. A B A G
re mi re do

6. F G A F
do re mi do

Resource Master 1•4, Page 5

1. **a.-b.** Beat 6 **d.-e.** Beat 3 **g.-h.** Beat 3

b.-c. Beat 4 **e.-f.** Beat 1

c.-d. Beat 6 **f.-g.** Beat 2

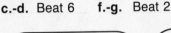

2. Both a. and b. should be circled.

3. Because the duration of each of the rhythms is one beat, any one rhythm can fill in any one of the blank spaces.

Resource Master 1•6, Page 7

Assessment A

1. a. 2. a. 3. d. 4. b. 5. d. 6. a.

Assessment B

1. c. 2. b. 3. a. 4. c. 5. c. 6. b.

Resource Master 2•1, Page 9

Lines should be drawn through "Raise your hand and ask." and "Al-li-ga-tors crawl."

Resource Master 2•2, Page 10

1a. do re mi so la
C D E G A

1b. so la so mi re do
G A G E D C

1c. do la so mi re
G E' D' B A

1d. la so do re mi so
E D G A B D

2. ATINNOMU = MOUNTAIN
6

RYLOG = GLORY
3

TINAR = TRAIN
4

NODBU = BOUND
5   1

MELCOWE = WELCOME
2

AGNUF = FUNGA
7

D	E	G	A	B	A	G
1	2	3	4	5	6	7

Resource Master 2•3, Page 11

Resource Master 2•3, Page 11

4. a.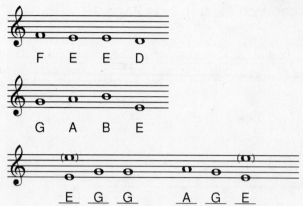

b.

c.

d.

Resource Master 2•4, Page 12

B E D

F A D E D

B E A D E D

D A D

C A D E

A C E

A D D

C A G E

F E E D

G A B E

E G G   A G E

Resource Master 2•5, Page 13

1. D.   **3.** E. or C.   **5.** A.

2. C. or E.   **4.** B.

6.   2 beat(s)

7.   4 beat(s)

8.   1 beat(s)

9.   3 beat(s)

10.   4 beat(s)

11.   2 beat(s)

Resource Master 2•6, Page 14

Assessment A

1. a.   **2.** b.   **3.** a.   **4.** c.

Assessment B

1. c.   **2.** a.   **3.** b.   **4.** d.

Answer Key

Resource Master 3•1, Page 19

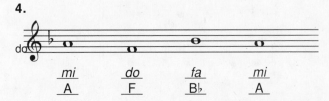
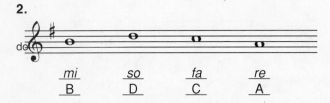
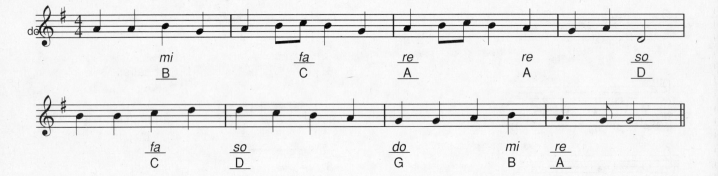

1.

do mi fa so
G B C D

3.

so fa mi do
G F E C

2.

mi so fa re
B D C A

4.

mi do fa mi
A F B♭ A

mi | fa | re | re | so
B | C | A | A | D

fa | so | do | mi | re
C | D | G | B | A

Resource Master 3•2, Page 20

1. Copland studied in Paris for three years.

2. Copland used American folk-song material to give his compositions an American flavor.

3. Billy the Kid, Rodeo, and Appalachian Spring are Copland's very popular ballets.

Resource Master 3•3, Page 21

1. a. **2.** c. **3.** d. **4.** b.

McGraw-Hill

Resource Master 3•5, Page 23

Assessment A

1. b.   **2.** a.   **3.** a.   **4.** a.   **5.** b.

Assessment B

1. a.   **2.** b.   **3.** b.   **4.** c.   **5.** c.

Resource Master 3•6, Page 24

1. Harriet decided to escape when she heard that she was going to be sold.

2. A conductor on the Underground Railroad helped transport enslaved people to freedom.

3. Answers will vary.

Resource Master 3•7, Pages 25-26

ACROSS	DOWN
2. Chorus	**1.** Moses
3. Score	**3.** Spirituals
4. Opera	**4.** Overture
7. Aria	**5.** Harriet Tubman
8. Baritone	**6.** Duet
13. Libretto	**9.** Recitative
14. Bass	**10.** Mezzo
15. Soprano	**11.** Tenor
17. Thea Musgrave	**12.** Librettist
18. The mouse	**16.** Alto

Resource Master 4•2, Page 30

1a. C major   **1b.** G major   **1c.** F major   **1d.** B♭ major   **1e.** D major

2. E♭ major

3. A major

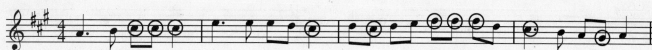

4.

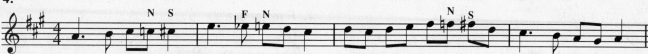

5.

6.

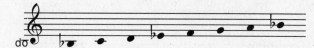

Answer Key

Resource Master 4•4, Page 32

1. b.   **2.** d.   **3.** a.   **4.** c.

5. Name the last three   months of the year. Oc - to - ber, No-vem-ber, De - cem - ber.

6. Who lives in the White House? The   pres - i - dent.

Resource Master 4•5, Page 33

3.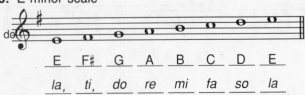

4.

5.    **8.**

6.   **9.**

7.   **10.**

Resource Master 4•6, Page 34

1. B minor scale

la, ti, do re mi fa so la
B   C♯   D   E   F♯   G   A   B

2. D minor scale

la, ti, do re mi fa so la
D   E   F   G   A   B♭   C   D

3. E minor scale

E   F♯   G   A   B   C   D   E
la, ti, do re mi fa so la

4. F major scale

F   G   A   B♭   C   D   E   F
do re mi fa so la ti do

5.

6.

Resource Master 4•7, Pages 35-37

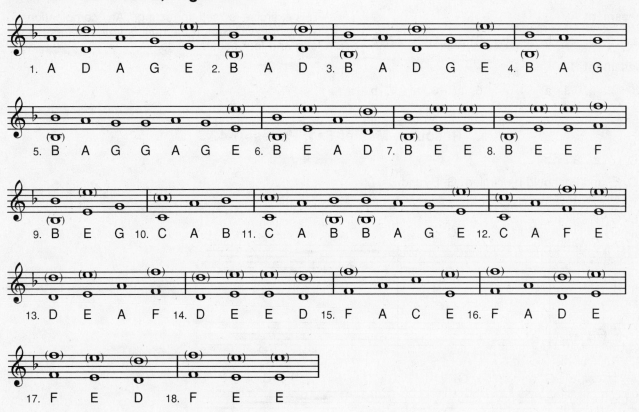

1. A D A G E 2. B A D 3. B A D G E 4. B A G

5. B A G G A G E 6. B E A D 7. B E E 8. B E E F

9. B E G 10. C A B 11. C A B B A G E 12. C A F E

13. D E A F 14. D E E D 15. F A C E 16. F A D E

17. F E D 18. F E E

A variety of words can be spelled in numbers 19
and 20. Here are some possibilities: ace, add,
age, bade, bed, cage, dad, edge, egg, fad, feed,
gab, gage.

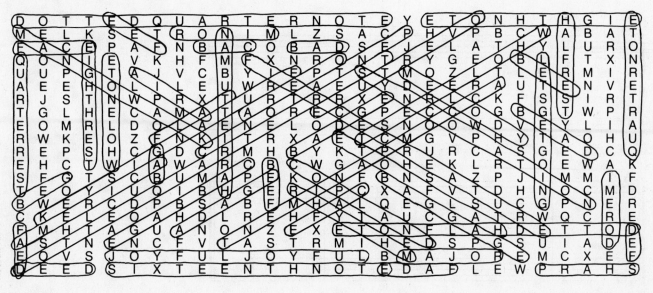

Answer Key

Resource Master 4•9, Page 39

Assessment A

1. a. 2. b. **3.** b. 4. c. **5.** a. **6.** b. 7. b.

Assessment B

1. b. **2.** a. **3.** a. **4.** a. **5.** a. **6.** a. 7. b.

Resource Master 4•10, Page 40

This exercise is "self-correcting." Any combination of rhythms will work if the quilt is four squares long and four squares wide.

Resource Master 5•1, Pages 41-42

1. C   **2.** G

3. C, E, and G should be circled. G, B, and D should be boxed.

4. C, G

Resource Master 5•4, Page 46

1. F, A, and C should be circled. C, E, and G should be boxed.

2. F, C

3.

Resource Master 5•7, Page 49

Assessment A

1. b. 2. a. 3. b. 4. b. 5. c. 6. a. 7. a.

Assessment B

1. a. 2. a. 3. b. 4. a. 5. b. 6. c. 7. d.

Resource Master 6•4, Page 56

Answers will vary.

Resource Master 6•7, Pages 60-62

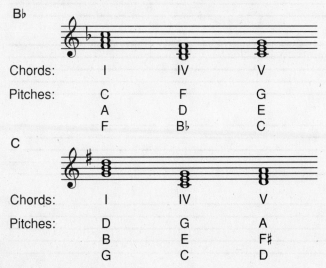

Check the spelling of the chords as follows: CEG, FAC, GBD, B♭DF.

Resource Master 6•10, Pages 65-66

Both pages of cards were designed so that before they're cut apart, each row of symbols matches the row of labels below it.

Resource Master 6•11, Page 67

Assessment A

1. d. 2. a. 3. b. 4. b. 5. c.

Assessment B

1. c. 2. c. 3. d. 4. a. 5. a.

Resource Master C•3, Page 73

1. John Philip Sousa began his military career in the United States Marine Band.

2. In 1889 the *Washington Post* asked Sousa to write a march named after the newspaper. It was to be played at their essay contest's awards ceremony.

3. Sousa wrote songs, waltzes, orchestral suites, tone poems, novels, and his autobiography, *Marching Along.*